Every Manager's Guide to Business Processes

Every Manager's Guide to Business Processes

A Glossary of Key Terms & Concepts for Today's Business Leader

Peter G.W. Keen
And
Ellen M. Knapp

Harvard Business School Press
Boston, Massachusetts

For my children, Sara and Chris,
and to the memory of Lucy
　　　　　　　—P. K.

For my children, Wendy and Robert,
and for my patient colleagues
　　　　　　　—E. K.

———◦◉◦———

00 99 98 97 96   5 4 3 2 1

Library of Congress Cataloging-in-Publication Data

Keen, Peter G. W.
　　Every manager's guide to business processes : a glossary of key
　terms & concepts for today's business leader / Peter G. W. Keen,
　Ellen M. Knapp.
　　　　p.　cm.
　　Includes index.
　　ISBN 0-87584-627-0 (hc)
　　ISBN 0-87584-575-4 (pbk)
　　1. Industrial management—Terminology
　　2. Business—Terminology.
I. Knapp, Ellen M.　II. Title.
HD30.17.K44　1995
650'.03—dc20　　　　　　　　　　　　　　　　95-16636
　　　　　　　　　　　　　　　　　　　　　　　　CIP

The paper used in this publication meets the requirements of the
American National Standard for Permanence of Paper for Printed
Library Materials Z39.49-1984.

Contents

Preface

This book is the equivalent of a guidebook to a country you are visiting. You probably know a fair amount about the country, worry a little about how to handle the foreign language, and want information that quickly, clearly, and reliably helps you decide which sights to see and how to find your way around. *Every Manager's Guide to Business Processes* aims to guide you through the world of business processes.

Every manager already has a broad understanding of the basics of total quality management, reengineering, downsizing, the learning organization, outsourcing, and other aspects of what we call process "movements"—the many concepts, rallying cries, and methodologies that have brought "business process" from mere occasional mention in the most influential management books of the 1920s to the late 1980s into the common parlance of today's business life. Every manager also knows that business processes have become a major, and for many companies even *the* major, element in competitive positioning. The 1990s have seen the most sustained commitment in the history of business to programs designed explicitly to establish a process advantage. Business processes have come to represent a country we all must visit regularly—one where we may even end up living. More than ever before, managers need a concise guide to the key concepts and terms that denote the lay of the land.

We consider *Every Manager's Guide to Business Processes* our translation of research and practice across the process movements, a selection of the terms and concepts that managers need to know in order to take effective action in what we call "Business Process Investment": choosing the right process to get right. Choosing this process requires understanding the nature of business processes, how to set priorities for improving them, and how to select the most appropriate methodology and tools. It also requires insight into the economic nature of processes, a topic almost entirely ignored by the process movements, which focus largely on the work flows of activities that constitute the most visible elements of a process.

Every Manager's Guide aims at helping our readers build that understanding and insight. Over the past three years, we have been working with a small group of colleagues on Business Process Investment. As we reviewed volumes of case examples of process innovation and examined the relevant research literature, we found that there was no established body of expertise or common language about business processes as a whole. There are plenty of specialized languages—those of total quality management, information technology, the learning organization, and reengineering, for instance. TQM talks about kaizen, fishbone diagrams, ISO 9000, PDCA, and the Deming cycle. The IT field's conception of business process innovation relies heavily on client/server, groupware, and UNIX front ends. The learning organization is built on the Fifth Discipline and systems thinking. Reengineering talks about case management and process owners. And there are terms directly relevant to exploiting the opportunity of business processes such as mass customization, the shamrock organization, transaction cost economics, negative working capital, economic value-added, core competences, and outsourcing. Interpreting even the *basic* vocabulary of business processes can challenge any manager, much less weeding out such esoteric terms as Rule of

Whacko, Big Hairy Audacious Goals, and Starburst enterprise as well as grappling with the lingo of many business fads that have grown up around the process movements, creating what Robert Johansen calls "bumper sticker thinking." The current managerial dilemma is that business processes are clearly key for understanding and acting, but it's hard to understand the business process field thoroughly and reliably enough to act effectively.

Hence this book. *Every Manager's Guide to Business Processes* offers very busy managers a simple, but not simplistic, review of key terms and concepts, focusing on exactly what they mean for business action and identifying just how *little* managers need to know. Sorting through the jargon, hype, vaguely defined terms, evangelism, and expansive claims that characterize the language of business process movements has been a challenge. We hope that in writing this guide we have helped create a clearing in the terminological forest.

That clearing gave us a better sense of the overall landscape. We winnowed down the many hundreds of terms to the roughly 100 that we feel fully cover the territory. Every manager will know some of them but may not have considered what they mean for Business Process Investment—that is, for taking action to get the right process right and thus create value for the firm, customers, and investors. And many managers may be familiar with the language and concepts of a particular process movement but want to broaden their vocabularies and thinking. Ironically, a fundamental tenet of TQM, the learning organization, the team-based organization, and reengineering is that firms must break away from the traditional hierarchy, division of labor, and functional organization to create the networked, collaborative, cross-functional company, yet these movements are highly compartmentalized in their thinking. The industrial engineering tradition that underlies TQM and reengineering, for instance, fails to draw on the many insights of the emerging mainstream thought and practice in corporate finance. Many books on reengineering are uninformed about leading work in corporate strategy and organizational behavior. Business strategists lack an understanding of information technology even when their recommendations depend on it. Those economists who understand the fundamentals of business processes as "firm-specific assets" and "dynamic capabilities" rarely refer to the proven business tools that turn their academic concepts into practical business tools.

Every Manager's Guide to Business Processes aims at providing managers with a comprehensive, cross-disciplinary summary of the fundamentals of business processes and business process innovation. The definitions herein constitute a universal language that will help managers traverse the territory.

Acknowledgments

This book is one of the outputs of a joint project carried out over a two-year period by Coopers & Lybrand and the International Center for Information Technologies. The goal of the project has been to develop practical tools for business process investment. The undertaking was innovative and stimulating, and involved some very creative people. Much of what we write in this book arose so directly from the team's joint thinking that it is impossible to sort out intellectual authorship.

Lynda Woodman, president of the International Center for Information Technologies, generated many key concepts, backed by her rich and practical experience as a manager. It was Lynda who pointed the research project toward viewing business processes as capital assets, a direction that became the base for the Business Process Investment framework which is the main result of our study. Without her creativity and managerial expertise, this book would have been diminished. Stan Raatz of Coopers & Lybrand provided a strong analytic and theoretical grounding for the intellectual underpinnings of our work. Joe Schlosser, Sherry Speakman, and others at Coopers improved and extended our work by applying it in a number of organizations. Larry Arnold turned the initial brainstorming exercise into a manageable project.

Each of us has individual thanks to add to our joint acknowledgments.

From Peter Keen

This is the sixth book (with another one in the works) for which Carol Franco has been my publisher and my fourth book with the Harvard Business School Press. Writing a book is the easy part; the tough part is turning it into something that people will want to read. Carol and her team at the Press care about books and treat them as something special, not just "product." For me as an author, their judgment, support, and expertise have been a key and much-valued resource.

From Ellen Knapp

Robert Johansen and his colleagues at the Institute for the Future took an early interest in our work and provided a forum for a broader discussion of our research. The ensuing dialog enriched our thinking and, as a result, the final product.

Every Manager's Guide to Business Processes

Introduction

This book is offered as a guide to managers who must navigate what has become one of the most important voyages in business today: creating a process advantage. Business processes—the manner in which work is organized, coordinated, and targeted to produce something of value—are increasingly recognized as a key not just to competitive success, but to competitive survival. What may be called process movements—business process reengineering, total quality management, the learning organization, time-based competition, the virtual corporation, and team-based organization are a few examples—have come to dominate management thought, and managers' bookshelves.

These movements reflect a major shift in business thinking and practice. Throughout past decades, management focus was on inputs, that is, strategy, and outputs, generally products and measurable results. This left the details of business processes to lower level operations staff. Today, this has given way to recognition that process matters, and that it is top management's responsibility to drive the radical changes in business processes that are dictated by an economy in which yesterday's success in no way guarantees today's viability. Some of these changes are to:

- Remove waste, delays, multiplicity of steps, and paperwork that mark many aspects of customer service and administration;

- Redesign processes, originally designed to meet internal needs, to address the needs and convenience and maximize the satisfaction of customers.

- Recognize that quality is a requirement for playing the game, not a premium for which an extra charge can be assessed.

- Break down the constraints of hierarchy, functional organization and structure, and traditional attitudes of "management knows best"; encourage flexibility, cross-functional coordination, and team collaboration. Recognize that the people who do the work know best and provide them with the authority and education they need to innovate and operate effectively.

- Use information technology—computers, telephones, telecommunications links, data bases, and so forth—not to automate existing processes, but to enable new forms of service and coordination.

- Recognize that time is the new currency of competitiveness; that time to market is a determinant of product success, and response time is a determinant of service success.

This is just part of the litany of demands being made upon business management today.

That business processes have assumed new and growing importance as competitive differentiators is readily illustrated. Consider the following representative examples of levels of improvement reported by firms in particular processes.

- Harley-Davidson cut product delivery time from 360 to 3 days.

- Citibank cut the time required to process a mortgage application from 30–60 days to 15 minutes.

- Ford slashed warranty costs per car from $1,100 to $100.

- Telecot, an agricultural trading organization, increased transactions per employee from 9,000 to 450,000 per year.
- Toyota increased annual asset turnover from 16 to 215 times.
- Florida Power and Light credits a total quality management program with reducing power outages per customer from 7 hours to 32 minutes per year.
- Hallmark Cards reengineered its product development from 2–3 years to less than 1 year.
- Taco Bell's elimination of management layers reduced area supervisors from 350 for 1,800 restaurants to 100 for 2,300 and boosted profits and market share.
- Bell Atlantic reduced from 15 to 3 days the time required to install new telecommunications circuits for businesses and cut associated labor costs from $88 million to $6 million.
- Many companies that substituted electronic data interchange for printed purchase orders and invoices cut costs per transaction from $10–60 to around 15 cents.

Most of these examples would have seemed fantasies in the 1970s and were unusual enough even into the late 1980s and 1990s to be heralded in books and articles as pioneering successes. Today they are commonplace. They demonstrate that organizations can make step shift and dramatic improvements in the basics of their business operations.

Because radical change has traditionally been impeded by "resistance" and "inertia," the most influential models of change management have stressed carefully phased implementation: unfreezing the status quo; facilitating momentum for change; and refreezing the equilibrium to institutionalize the change. Radical change guided by such models has rarely succeeded.

Mainstream business thinking today favors radicalism, of necessity. Firms cannot tinker their way to survival, never mind success. Process movements, whether business process reengineering, by far the most aggressive philosophy of radical change, or total quality management, which pursues radical change through continuous incremental improvement, establish new competitive targets that will be out of reach of companies that choose not to try to dramatically improve their process performance.

Process-Driven Competition

The dramatic levels of improvement cited above are also a warning: once new levels of process capability become the norm, firms stuck at the old levels or willing to make only incremental improvements risk going out of business. Industry process leaders are almost always its premium service providers and low-cost producers. Whatever the service—banking, auto repair, transportation, retailing, insurance, travel, telephone—whoever the providers of the everyday products you use—consumer electronics, household items, major appliances—what differentiates the best from the average is not so much product or service *features,* but the overall experience of dealing with the firm in terms of reliability, quality, consistency, ease of ordering, responsiveness to queries and problems, and so forth. Compare price and the best often match or beat the average. Same features, same or better price, *and* something "extra" or "different."

The something extra or different is process advantage. Study after study reveals far more differences in firms' economic performance as measured by long-term return on assets *within* an industry than across industries and relates those differences directly to business processes. A widely cited field study of 18 air conditioning manufacturers found, for example, that performance differences were related not to level of capital investment or degree of automation, but to what the authors described as "organizational routines" that had an impact on coordination. Leaders and laggards that compete in the same market with essentially the same products at comparable prices vary by as much as a factor of eight in measures of performance. As oligopolies such as the U.S. auto industry have had to respond to aggressive competition, as a growing number of industries faces overcapacity and commoditization, as deregulation and globalization remove protective barriers to entry, and as customer loyalty is increasingly won by service excellence, these differences have continued to grow, with the leaders exploiting and the laggards ignoring opportunities for process improvement.

What is behind most of the ascensions from membership to pack leadership over the past two decades—Wal-Mart's surpassing of Sears and Kmart through the streamlining of store replenishment processes; Dell's preemption of personal computer retailing through radical improvements in order, assembly, and delivery processes; American Airlines' dominance of TWA, Eastern, Continental, and other previously stronger national carriers through innovations in reservations, marketing, and profit management processes; and the regional success Southwest Airlines has built on deviations from standard industry route planning, pricing, and employee relations processes—is mostly process-related. The same process-driven leader-laggard gaps are in evidence in banking, insurance, publishing, and manufacturing, among other industries. Even product differentiation is today short-lived and less dependent on a particular product than on the product development process. Studies have shown that a premium product on the market typically garners as much as 60 percent market share and is seldom displaced by a comparable later product. Good products late cannot compete against good products fast, and good products accompanied by poor service and well-designed but poor-quality products cannot compete for long, if at all.

Why *Every Manager's Guide*?
Business process reengineering is the most recent, total quality management the most well-established, of the process movements.

Within these, and among other process movements that emphasize time-based competition and virtual, team-based, shamrock, and learning organizations, there are many flavors.

Each movement has its own conceptions, terms, and tools promulgated to managers in books, articles, consulting methodologies, and claims and case examples that range from silly to substantive, from hyperbolic to realistic. Overselling of this year's Idea of the Century is matched only by excesses in the coining of vaguely defined terms and promotion of jargon. From the total quality management movement we have the House of Quality, fishbone diagrams, and Taguchi methods; from business process reengineering/redesign/innovation we have case manager, workflow, and process owner and modeling; from the organizational process redesign movement we have new definitions of such common words as collaborate, coordinate, team, and network as well as novel notions conveyed by words such as spiderweb, shamrock, and worknet; from information technology, notorious for its mind-numbing jargon and acronyms, we have client/server, workstation, and architecture.

Hence this guide. In subsequent sections of this Introduction we consider (1) what constitutes a business process, (2) evidence for business process as critical to competitive positioning, (3) process movements, and (4) Business Process Investment, a framework for getting the right process right, that is, for identifying process opportunities and choosing the process that most effectively builds value. These discussions are intended to orient readers to a very broad topic.

The selective Glossary presented here goes beyond dictionary-style definitions to highlight the managerial relevance of each term. "Definitions" of the terms in the Glossary vary in length from a paragraph to a few pages; some include cross-references to other relevant definitions.

Every Manager's Guide to Business Processes defines all significant terms from the process movements that have most influenced business thought and practice. These vary widely in conception and recommendation, particularly regarding focus on radical change (reengineering's "start with a clean sheet of paper") or on incremental change (total quality management's continuous improvement), relative emphasis on workflows and those who perform them as the driver of process change, and whether technology or organization is the principal enabler of change.

This guide is based on four observations.

1. There is ample evidence that business process is a major, often *the* major, source of sustainable competitive differentiation, particularly in "commodity" industries characterized by little product or service differentiation, aggressive price competition, and overcapacity (banking, retailing, airlines, consumer electronics, insurance, and much of manufacturing are among such industries).

2. The process movements, business process redesign/reengineering and total quality management in particular, have led to immense improvements in process performance in many and varied firms. It is this demonstrated capacity that is referred to here as "getting a process right."

3. There is also ample evidence that getting the process right does not necessarily ensure a firm's success or guarantee an economic payoff. This is the process paradox.

4. To exploit a process opportunity and avoid the process paradox is to "get the right process right."

To help managers get the right process right, this book provides them with a process language, a process investment framework, and a process investment tool kit. Most important is a process language. The language we use to think and talk about a business process determines the domain of possibilities for practical action. These possibilities are today constrained by (1) experience and knowledge that make it difficult for skilled managers to think about business processes in other than very broad terms (e.g., "product development" or "manufacturing") or the highly specific workflows and activities involved in producing a product and generating an invoice; (2) rigid views of business processes and process improvement that impede skilled managers' understanding of other views and, hence, other ways of improving processes (examples might include advocates of reengineering who are unfamiliar with total quality management and vice-versa); (3) confusion and frustration on the part of skilled managers by the jargon, particularly as related to the use of technology, that tends to be promulgated by process movements; and (4) skilled managers' lack of understanding of the range of opportunities for process innovation and improvement.

The emphasis in this list on *skilled* managers is meant to suggest that the problem for managers in general is not so much competence or capability (notwithstanding the opening diatribes about American management with which some best-selling books introduce otherwise useful discussions of process issues) but rather not knowing what they don't know. This guide is intended to acquaint these managers with the key ideas and terms they need in order to focus their skills on business process opportunities.

The second element in getting the right process right, a comprehensive framework for process investment, goes beyond process improvement or process change, which involves primarily getting processes right. Getting the right process right requires a basis for zeroing in on the most promising opportunities and not wasting resources on projects that, however attractive on the surface, do not create substantial value for the firm and, hence, its customers and shareholders (construed here to be owners of pension funds, IRAs, and mutual funds as well as stockholders).

The Business Process Investment framework, developed with colleague Ellen Knapp and a small team that included Lynda Woodman and Stan Raatz, is introduced here to encourage managers to think about process opportunities more generally and to view process investment as independent of any of a priori commitment to any one process movement's solutions. In leading managers in a search for process improvements that matter to their firms' success, either as today's opportunity or tomorrow's necessity or potential breakthrough, *Every Manager's Guide to Business Processes* goes beyond language and terms to concepts and applications.

The process investment tool kit offered here is a product of the authors' consulting experience. It was assembled by stepping back from the many advocacies and claims of the various process movements to evaluate how the tools employed in successful process improvements might be usefully applied in other contexts and whether there exist patterns of success that suggest a general-purpose tool kit. What can we learn from total quality management (TQM), for example, that might be applied to any process under any banner? In the authors' work experience, managers did not need to understand in depth, for example, the proven tools of total quality management just as it is not necessary, generally, for people engaged in TQM initiatives to understand, in depth, information technology or corporate finance.

The hallmarks of the process view advanced here are: business as cross-functional, team-centered, coordination; communication as preferable to command and control; and old assumptions challenged, not reinforced. This book provides managers with the requisites for embracing this view: a process language for thinking about and discussing processes; an investment framework for selecting opportunities; and a tool kit for turning opportunities into action.

The Process Paradox

The process paradox is succinctly summarized in a report of a study conducted in 1993 by McKinsey and Company of business process reengineering projects in 100 companies.

> In all too many companies, reengineering has been not only a great success but also a great failure. After months, even years,

of careful redesign, these companies achieve dramatic improvements in individual processes only to watch overall results decline. By now, paradoxical outcomes of this kind have become
almost commonplace. A computer company reengineers its finance department, reducing process costs by 34%—yet operating income stalls. An insurer cuts claims process time by 44%—
yet profits drop. Managers proclaim a 20% cost reduction, a
25% quality improvement—yet in the same period, business-
unit costs increase and profits decline. (Gene Hall, Jim Rosen-
thal, and Judy Wade, "How to Make Reengineering *Really* Work,"
Harvard Business Review, November–December 1993, 119.)

There are many other testaments to the process paradox. General
Motors and IBM, for instance, won through the implementation
of total quality management initiatives the prestigious Baldrige
award for quality at the very time that their economic and competitive performance was plummeting. And the insurance company that launched its reengineering movement with an initiative
that reduced its policy issuing process from three weeks to two to
four hours wound up insolvent and was taken over by state regulators a few months later.

Stated simply, the process paradox is that immense benefits
do not necessarily translate into business value. Less paradoxical,
but equally alarming in terms of wasted resources and disap-
pointed expectations, is the widely acknowledged proportion of
reengineering projects that fail: 50–70%. Surveys of total quality
management programs suggest a comparable failure rate.

Taken together, the process paradox and rate of implementation failure constitute a dire warning. The reasons business managers must come to grips with the details of business processes are
obvious: given the benefit side of paradox—the potential levels of
improvement in costs, time, and staffing—no manager can afford
to overlook process improvement opportunities; managers must
first know how to choose the' right process if they are to get the
process right (every explanation of the process paradox ties failure to widespread inability to identify, and therefore invest in,

process improvement that has a positive impact on overall business, economic, and organizational health); if theirs are not to number among the more than half of process improvement projects that fail, with attendant wastes of effort and money, managers, having chosen the right process, must be able to get it right.

This book advises managers to choose first the right process to get right and then an appropriate process value builder, a program of action that ranges from abandoning the process, to streamlining it, to outsourcing it, to making it a product, to turning it into a franchise, or to using it to preempt competitors in other industries. It treats processes not as workflows, but as invisible economic assets and liabilities. Some will be identity processes that define a firm and determine how investors and customers view it, some will be priority processes, others will be what we term background processes, necessary to business operations, but not directly involved in the creation of economic value. Much of the process paradox derives, we believe, from the tendency of reengineering aficionados to select background liability processes for repair and equate benefits with value. *Every Manager's Guide to Business Processes* explores the full range of process movements, grouping definitions in a manner that corresponds to our Business Process Investment framework. The list of process value builders included here in the definitions of terms, for example, is to our knowledge the first systematic summary of the specific proven options available to firms for process improvement. This book presents a comprehensive and focused review of what business managers need to know to make informed decisions about process investment that generates competitive advantage, organizational responsiveness to the forces of change, and economic value.

What Is a Business Process?

There are two somewhat different interpretations of business process among the process movements. One is of a process as a workflow, a series of activities aimed at producing something of value, the other, of a process as the coordination of work, whereby a set of skills and routines is exploited to create a capability that cannot be easily matched by others.

Annotated observations pertaining to both interpretations are presented below. From the workflow tradition we have the following.

- "We define a business process as a collection of activities that takes one or more kind of inputs and creates an output that is of value to the customer" (Michael Hammer and James Champy, *Reengineering the Corporation: A Manifesto for Business Revolution* [New York: HarperBusiness, 1993], 35). This, the industrial engineer's conception of process, neglects entirely leadership, cultural, incentive, management development, and other processes that lack well-defined inputs, outputs, and activities. One of the shortcomings of business process reengineering is that its emphasis on processes with well-defined workflows can lead managers to overlook processes of far greater consequence to their firms' economic and organizational health. Recall General Motors' failures in leadership and labor relations processes, which offset its many investments in new manufacturing processes.

- "A process is a structured, measured set of activities designed to produce a specified output for a particular customer or market. . . . A process is thus a specific ordering of work activities across time and space, with a beginning, an end, and clearly identified inputs and outputs: a structure for action" (Thomas H. Davenport, *Process Innovation: Reengineering Work through Information Technology* [Boston: Harvard Business School Press, 1993], 5). This, too, is the industrial engineering conception; what about crisis management, team building, and other processes that are neither structured nor measurable?

- "A process is a set of linked activities that take an input and transform it to an output" (Henry J. Johansson et al., *Business Process Re-engineering: Breakpoint Strategies for Market Dominance* [New York: John Wiley & Sons, 1993]).

- "A business process is most broadly defined as an activity that carries out a series of steps, which produces a specific result or a related series of results" (Daniel Morris and Joel Brandon, *Reengineering Your Business* [New York: McGraw-Hill, 1993]).

- "We assume that all processes can be thought of as a set of activities (e.g., 'steps,' 'tasks,' or 'subprocesses')" (Thomas W. Malone, Kevin Crowston, Jintae Lee, and Brian Petland, "Tools for Inventing Organizations: Toward a Handbook of Organizational Processes," working paper #141, MIT Center for Coordination Science, Sloan School of Management, Cambridge, Mass., May 1993).

- "Process: a series of operations linked together to provide a result that has increased value. . . . Process improvement: activities employed to detect and remove common causes of variation in order to improve process capability." (Warren H. Schmidt and Jerome P. Finnegan, *The Race without a Finish Line: America's Quest for Total Quality* [San Francisco: Jossey-Bass, 1992], 350–51). Note here a distinguishing feature of the total quality management movement: a focus on removing variation and ensuring that process outputs meet a target.

These observations and definitions highlight the emphasis of this interpretation of process on the existence of clearly delineated inputs and outputs, most obviously products, the target of the total quality management movement (TQM), and services and transaction processes that involve managing extensive paper flows, the principal targets of business process reengineering (BPR).

Now consider these contrasting observations and definitions steeped in the interpretation of process as coordination.

- "The real sources of advantage are to be found in management's ability to consolidate corporatewide technologies and production skills into competences that empower individual businesses to adapt quickly to changing opportunities" (C.K. Prahalad and Gary Hamel, "The Core Competence of the Corporation," *Harvard Business Review,* May–June 1990, 81).

- "A distinctive competence is a set of differentiated skills, complementary assets, and organizational routines which together allow a firm to coordinate a particular set of activities in a way that provides the basis for competitive advantage in a particular market or markets" (David J. Teece, Gary Pisano, and Amy Shuen, "Dynamic Capabilities and Strategic Management," working paper #90-8, Consortium on Competition and Cooperation, Center for Research in Management, University of California, Berkeley, 1992, 22).

- "Rather than tracking the flow of materials or data, business processes chart the coordination of action between people (and sometimes machines) involved in an activity" (Fernando Flores, "Offering New Principles for a Shifting Business World" [Business Design Associates, Emeryville, Calif., 1991], 21).

The difference between these interpretations is to some extent one of relative emphasis on process improvement. Moreover, one builds on the other. The interpretation of process as coordination complements that of process as workflows and activities, adding consideration of teams, collaboration, and coordination and an emphasis on factors that yield a "dynamic organizational capability" or "core competence" that is not easily matched by competitors. It equates business process with a combination of technologies and skills. That many of the definitions of business process within what might be termed the coordination (in contrast to the workflow) tradition tend to be academic and even a little elliptic can lead to their insights being overlooked.

At one level, the precise definition of business process may not matter. Indeed, to the foregoing definitions we can usefully add a third, more commonsensical definition: "any aspect of organizational functioning to which the word *process* can meaningfully be added." Given how commonsensically important leadership and capital resource allocation processes are, for example, why adopt a definition of them that excludes them from a firm's opportunity list?

Regardless of definition, business process implies (1) organization of work to achieve a result; (2) multiple steps and coordination of people; (3) an element of design or implementation that renders a business process as distinctive a competitive asset as research and development or product development, a "firm-specific asset" (in the words of institutional economists), "core competence," or "dynamic capability"; and (4) management as the enabler and sustainer of process advantage.

What matters about the choice of definition is that it is attended by a whole set of preconceptions and expectations that can strongly influence managers' thinking. Business process reengineering devotees, for example, are naturally inclined to think of investment opportunities as processes characterized by complex administrative workflows and to view improvement in terms of radical rethinking and streamlining with the aid of information technologies such as groupware, image processing, and front-end workstations. They likely have not even considered other types of processes and other types of process value builders. Managers familiar with and committed to total quality management, on the other hand, may not be aware of the process value builders reengineering has so successfully exploited, hubbing, for example (i.e., enabling a single case manager to handle electronically an entire customer service transaction as an alternative to moving paper through a series of departments). In both instances what we have is a specific interpretation of process blocking broader process insight.

Process Insight

Helping managers to develop process insight is the principal aim of this guide. It was process insight that led the State of Maryland to appropriate banking's automated teller machine capabilities to handle welfare benefits payments, that enabled British Airways to usurp control of the international hotel chains' own product by bundling hotel with airline reservations processes in a way that the hotels could not duplicate, that was the basis of FedEx's hubbing through a single national location the small package cargo traffic that the large airlines viewed as an add-on to passenger traffic over their point-to-point routes, that underlay Dell Computer's invention of the personal computer ordering and delivery processes that made it one of the fastest ever startup firms to reach $1 billion in revenues. The point to be made is that traditional thinking about business and organization is pointless in this highly nontraditional era of globalization, customer power, change as the norm, and process as advantage.

Traditional thinking about business processes is process blindness. It has marked most companies for decades, largely because managers have not had to pay attention to processes. This excerpt from a 1994 article in *Information Week* about a company that was for decades among the leading innovators in the computer industry could well have been written about a great many other firms.

> At the end of the three-hour meeting, [the chairman of the firm] sat back in his chair with a stunned look on his face. . . . "What you're telling me is the senior managers in this company that are making commitments to me have no idea how the company operates?"
>
> "On an operational level," [the executive responsible for business process redesign] remembers responding, "that's exactly what I'm telling you. . . . [I]t's no different at most companies. That is, senior managers don't know how their company con-

ducts its business operations. Real operational performance is no longer understood."

Making the Process View the Natural View

Most managers have not had to know much about business processes. The hierarchy looked after them and tradition determined how they were designed and executed. Managers focused on strategy, planning, organization, and market and product innovation. Only when all of these became process flavored, process centered, or process dominated were managers pressed to take a fresh look at their firms' business processes and make business process investment their own responsibility. To do this, they need sources of insight. Advocates and gurus of the process movements afford a partial perspective. *Every Manager's Guide to Business Processes* attempts to impart a broad view of the whole territory.

Among the greatest practical hurdles to developing process insight is the business mindset that views operations in terms of functions. For example, one major organization that committed enormous resources to process innovation, when it conducted a large-scale analysis of its business processes, arrived at an inventory that was little more than a list of activities within each unit (e.g., "sales support," "recruitment," "inventory management"). The dozens of teams and hundreds of people involved in making the inventory had no process language, only the language of departments, functions, job responsibilities, and budgets. It's hard to think in terms of process in an organization in which work is built around definitions of a particular part of a process. Business processes tend to be cross-functional, business organizational structure to be bounded by function.

The traditions of process as workflow and process as coordination attack the narrow functional view of work and the conceptions of organization that underlie it: reliance on hierarchy, division of labor, structural rigidity, limited worker authority, specialized job definitions and training, and department-centered budgets, incentives, and promotions. The workflow view is cross-functional, looking at the end-to-end process. The collaborative view similarly focuses on all the interactions, regardless of departmental boundaries. To break away from the functional view and make the process view a natural way of thinking, it is necessary to pose, and answer, the following questions.

1. Whenever the label "process" is attached to something (e.g., product development, capital budgeting, production), who *exactly* is the "customer," that is, the person or community to which the outcome matters?

2. What must happen for the customer's request or need to be satisfied? What value is (or should be created) by the process for the customer?

3. Who does the work? Who must work together?

4. How is the work to be coordinated?

5. Can information technology be exploited to improve coordination? Redesign the activities? Empower the people who do the work? Augment training? Alter incentives?

These questions marry the workflow and coordination traditions. They look at process, not function or activity. They ignore historical design and coordination. They do not prejudge the solution—perhaps the most effective value builder is a demonstrated tool of TQM, or perhaps the radical spirit of reengineering is more apposite—wait before you decide.

What Is the Evidence for Business Process as Critical to Competitive Positioning?

Unless, of course, it makes a difference to managers' impact on business performance, there is no need for process insight. Historically, it has not been a managerial necessity. Examine the index of any leading business book published before the late 1980s and you will find neither the term "process" nor its variants.

"Quality" rarely appears either, and then only as "quality circles," a popular but relatively short-lived business innovation of the 1970s. How is it that business process innovation/redesign/reengineering has become such a central element in firms' plans for the 1990s? Is process this and that to be just another short-lived fad, to be enthusiastically adopted and then largely forgotten together with Excellence, Theory Z, the strategic barnyard, and other hot items of the past two decades?

Faddishness, overselling, and hype notwithstanding, the new management focus on business processes seems to be well grounded. Here is a sampling of the evidence that business processes are a major source of competitive positioning and differentiation.

- Field studies document striking differences in economic performance and quality among companies that employ equivalent technology and produce equivalent products. The analysis of air conditioner manufacturers mentioned earlier found assembly line defects in U.S. plants to range from 8 to 165 per hundred units (more than one defect per unit for some manufacturers!), a huge span until one considers that between U.S. and Japanese companies, best to worst for the latter ranges from 0.15 to 3 per hundred units.

- In every industry studied, when information technology changes the basics of core logistics, 50 percent of firms disappear within a decade, among them several of the top ten performers, for want of sufficiently early or effective investment in new process capability. Examples include airlines' computerized reservations systems, point of sale and quick response in retailing, and electronic data interchange in distribution. Only six of the top twenty discount chains in 1980 were still in business in 1990. An estimated 75 percent of distributors in the hospital and pharmacy health product supply industry went out of business as the three leaders made computer-to-computer ordering processes the norm.

- Process predators who become the new leaders by exploiting information technology to offer the same product without the existing infrastructures and process base often come from outside the industry. Examples include Fidelity Investments (a securities firm) and USAA (an insurance company), which offer full-service banking with no bank branches; Dell, which preempted existing computer retailers with full-service retailing sans stores; and FedEx, which snatched business that had been the province of the airlines and UPS. When predators can offer better service at lower operating and capital cost, the old process base is no longer an inherent asset.

- Companies that have a measurable time edge over their competition (in product development, order to delivery, manufacturing cycle time, and so forth) grow at about three times, and their profits at twice, the rate of their average competitors.

- Manufacturing firms typically spend 15 to 20 cents of every sales dollar redressing quality problems and other sources of customer complaint; the leaders in quality management report figures of less than one cent.

Most of these examples, being well over a decade old, are hardly "news." Why then is the business process view so recent? Why is it not in the indexes of the books that most influenced management theory and practice through the mid-1980s?

Part of the answer is that much of business process innovation and reengineering is not at all new, but derives from well-established industrial engineering methods. Some critics deem it little more than a modern form of "Taylorism," the Scientific Management discipline of the 1920s, in many ways the first process movement, that embraced rationalization of workflows, standards, and efficiency. The quality management movement's equally deep and long roots in business history also emanate from industrial engineering. Other elements of organizationally focused process movements that emphasize teams and networks are direct byproducts of mainstream work in organizational theory that dates back many decades. At one level, then, the new focus on business process is partly a confluence of well-established themes and fields, with updated labels and rallying cries.

But the search for the roots of process improvement doesn't answer the question "Why now?" Are the business process movements on to something about management that has hitherto eluded scholars and practitioners? Is there something about today's business environment that makes the process perspective more relevant to success?

What there are are new insights, most notably that information technology changes the basics of activity coordination. Telecommunications is making teamwork and customer service increasingly location-independent; enabling paper, the organizational enemy, to be moved electronically instead of physically; providing for customers to be served at their own moment of value (ordering goods, applying for loans, checking account status) via telephone or workstation; and facilitating the processing by a single "case manager" at a computer workstation of work previously routed through many departments.

Most important, information technology affects what is most fundamental to organizations: coordination costs versus transaction costs. Because historically this topic has been debated in theoretical economics journals, few managers are aware of it. Yet it is a powerful concept that won its originator a Nobel Prize for economics, albeit forty years after he advanced the idea. Asking the deceptively simple question "Why do firms exist at all?" Ronald Coase argued that the firm and the marketplace are alternate modes for organizing the same transaction, that is, the choice is make or buy. The decentralized market provides goods and services for a price: the transaction cost. Entities, that is, firms, can organize to produce goods for a coordination, or process, cost. (See Ronald H. Coase, "The Nature of the Firm," in *The Nature of the Firm: Origins, Evolution, and Development,* ed. Oliver E. Williamson and Sidney G. Winter [New York: Oxford University Press, 1993], ch. 2.)

If it can produce a good for less than the going price in the market, a firm will create internal processes ("hierarchies," in the language of transaction cost economics). If its coordination costs exceed the market price (transaction cost), it will buy the service outside or, if its own costs are higher, go out of business over the long term. Decisions about the basics of business processes that can differentiate firms thus depend on a comparison of the cost of coordinating activities associated with the factors of production and customer service *within* the firm with the costs of bringing about the same result through either market transactions or arrangements with another firm.

The essence of business process is coordination of the design and management of workflows (the industrial engineering tradition); investments in organizational resources such as people, structure, and strategy; and the costs of meeting target standards for quality and service. Management, research and development, and support functions are all elements of effective coordination of a business's processes.

Information technology is transforming coordination costs. A firm that reengineers customer service processes to provide fifteen-minute per transaction one-stop shopping via an "800" telephone number is selling the same "product" via an entirely new process. The same holds when a company links to its suppliers for automatic computer-to-computer ordering via electronic data interchange—same product, new process. A decision to outsource a function such as information technology data centers or distribution would consider the cost of internal management (coordination) relative to contracting out (transaction), taking into account the potentially significant coordination costs associated with managing the contractual relationship, which may well offset any price advantage. A firm that enters into an alliance with another firm incurs coordination costs. When a firm downsizes, the aim is, or should be, not to cut costs, but to cut the cost of coordinating a process without sacrificing performance.

It is because there are so many approaches to coordinating business processes, with information technology a major enabler of dramatic change, that so much of the process movements' ideas seem at once old and new. Information technology will be used by the workflow tradition to replace people, by the coordination tradition to augment their capabilities. Both aim for improved coordination.

Situational forces are also driving the new process perspective. In many ways, the process movements represent the rediscovery of work. The total quality management movement drew attention to workflows. The success of Japanese companies led to an emphasis on quality and teams. In manufacturing, continued reduction of direct labor as a percentage of costs has made analysis of systems flows central to work design. In fighting their way back into international markets, large U.S. firms have eliminated much egregious waste through downsizing, outsourcing, and reengineering, and stimulated a view of productivity as process determined and not just output based.

Information technology, the need to eliminate waste, and the focus on new modes of coordination are interdependent; each fuels the others. The pressures of change add momentum, pushing companies to fundamentally reevaluate the basics. It is no coincidence that the appearance of "business process" in the indexes of management books coincides with that of the "re-" words such as reengineering, restructure, reposition, reinvent, redesign. "Re-" means try again; it is a signal that things are not working.

Firms cannot control globalization, customer requirements, commoditization of and overcapacity in many industries, or social change, nor can they slow the pace of change. But they *can* control their own business processes. The purpose of this book is to help them figure out how.

Process Movements

Business process improvement relies on a combination of directional forces to build momentum for taking charge of change: top-down, senior management must define strategic direction and evidence its commitment and sustained leadership; middle-out, cross-functional teams must be employed to break down functional boundaries and barriers; and bottom-up, those who do the work and, hence, know more about it and how to improve it than do most managers must be empowered to serve as levers for major change. The need for change gave rise to a number of process movements during the 1980s and 1990s. These fall into fairly distinct groups, each characterized by specific features and philosophies. They are differentiated primarily by (1) the extent to which they espouse immediate radical versus continuous incremental change as the path to transformation, (2) the emphasis they place on workflows versus on the people who handle them as the primary focus of programs to improve processes, and (3) the breadth of their recommendations for action and, hence, the types of business processes they target for management attention and action.

Influential process movements are summarized below, together with their key themes and representative books.

Total Quality Management

This, the most well-established process movement, exists in several variants that share a common focus on:

1. continuous improvement of processes and zealous commitment to customers;

2. reduction in output variability in relation to a target standard that is both the principal goal and measure of quality;

3. reliance on the collection and analysis of statistical data to ensure "management by fact"; and

4. a rigorous set of disciplines backed by equally rigorous education of workers, supervisors, and managers in the principles and practice of quality management.

Most advocates of total quality management, or TQM, are disciples of W. E. Deming or Joseph Juran, the founders who individually (and often competitively) introduced the discipline into Japan during the 1950s. Japan has supplied many of the most effective concepts and tools of modern TQM, Toyota's Taiichi Ohno having made in the areas of lean production, kaizen, and just-in-time inventory (his invention) contributions that can only be described as genius.

Japan's successful exploitation of TQM is itself evidence of the immense impact of business processes on competitive positioning. So are the comebacks of American companies such as Ford and Xerox, which were built on, to use Ford's term, making quality Job 1.

Management readings: Philip Crosby, *Quality Is Free: The Art of Making Quality Free* (Milwaukee, Wisc.: American Society for Quality Control, 1979); W. Edwards Deming, *Out of the Crisis* (Milwaukee, Wisc.: American Society for Quality Control, 1986); Joseph M. Juran, *Juran on Planning for Quality* (Milwaukee, Wisc.: American Society for Quality Control, 1988).

Business Process Redesign/Innovation/ Reengineering

The many books and consulting methodologies that rely on a selective exploitation of information technology to improve business processes view process explicitly in terms of workflows and view industrial engineering equally explicitly as the discipline most relevant to the tools and principles of redesign. BPR stands for Business Process Redesign *and* Reengineering, the two being closely related both in origin (the academic banks of Cambridge's Charles River) and underlying approaches to process analysis and improvement. They are distinguished principally by attitude toward change, redesign/innovation tending to be less insistent on the fundamental destruction and rebuilding of existing processes. BPR is essentially industrial engineering updated to exploit the opportunities afforded by computers and telecommunications.

Reengineering is by far the most influential, and most controversial, recent process movement. It espouses radical change in business processes as a matter of survival for companies and targets dysfunctional, "broken" processes for investment. Reengineering proposes starting with a clean sheet of paper and asking "If we were to start this company now, how would we design the target process?" Reengineering's major process opportunity is the cross-functional streamlining of work activities; it attacks division of labor and consequent organization of work along functional boundaries as the single most constraining factor in customer service and efficiency. Most organizations' implementations of "reengineering" are closer in spirit to BPR, experts tending to differ about the practicality, necessity, and ethics of the reengineering credo "don't automate—obliterate."

Management readings: Thomas H. Davenport, *Process Innovation: Reengineering Work Through Information Technology* (Boston: Harvard Business School Press, 1993); Michael Hammer, "Reengineering Work: Don't Automate, Obliterate," *Harvard Business Review,* July–August 1990, 104–112; Michael Hammer and James Champy, *Reengineering the Corporation: A Manifesto for Business Revolution* (New York: HarperBusiness, 1993).

Time-Based Competition

Time is a recurring theme in many of the process movements, the focus being on how to reduce process cycle time as the key to cost, service, product leadership, and logistics. There are many variants on this theme: just-in-time concepts dominate manufacturing; quick response concepts dominate retailing; and time-based strategies, products, and services dominate banking.

Management reading: George Stalk, Jr., and Thomas M. Hout, *Competing Against Time: How Time-based Competition Is Reshaping Global Markets* (New York: Free Press, 1990).

The Learning Organization

Manufacturing has historically been governed by the management principle: workers do, managers think. This tenet is the essence of industrial engineering as embodied in Taylor's Scientific Management, assembly line and mass production techniques, and much of labor-management relationships.

Most of the process movements, implicitly if not explicitly, call for workers to think and managers to respect their knowledge, encourage their interest and commitment, and empower their autonomy and action. Business process innovation would have firms meet the forces of change with multiskilled workers in organizations structurally and culturally suited to collaboration and flexible adaptation. Knowledge is the foundation of organizational capabilities in these "learning" organizations, "adhocracies," "intelligent enterprises," "worknets," and variants thereof.

The learning organization (a term popularized by professor Peter Senge in *The Fifth Discipline*) is an ideal; it represents the desired direction for most large firms. Reengineering emphasizes work design, the learning organization the people side of process innovation, but both share the strongly held belief that radical rethinking is needed to break away from existing assumptions, beliefs, and attitudes. By most accounts, the creation and use of knowledge will be the basis for leadership and investment in people in the effective organization of tomorrow. Companies will be much smaller in size and with many fewer, but more highly skilled, jobs and need to make continued investment in developing new skills.

Management readings: James Brian Quinn, *Intelligent Enterprise*

(New York: Free Press, 1992); Peter M. Senge, *The Fifth Discipline: The Art and Practice of the Learning Organization* (New York: Doubleday/Currency, 1990).

Team-Based Organization

Teams are widely assumed to surpass individuals in most aspects of work, "self-managed" teams to be the building blocks of the flexible and collaborative organization. The traditional, functional structures that dominate most firms today are being replaced by teams among fast-growing start-ups, small businesses, and knowledge-centered units such as research and development and consulting teams. Division of labor makes a great deal of sense for routinized activities in a stable environment but is a poor base for dealing with change and uncertainty. Hence, in the neat phrase of two writers on the topic, the wisdom of teams. Although process innovation relies on teams, proponents of total quality management and business process redesign/reengineering frequently underestimate the disciplines involved in making teams more than a commonsense notion of people working together toward a shared goal.

Management reading: Jon R. Katzenbach and Douglas K. Smith, *The Wisdom of Teams: Creating the High-Performance Organization* (Boston: Harvard Business School Press, 1993).

The Networked Organization

The concept of "organization" has historically presumed a physical entity with a formal structure, facilities, stable operations, and most functions performed in-house. As it is rendered by circumstances increasingly obsolete, this concept is becoming the exception rather than the norm. Organizations are becoming more and more networks of relationships, with many functions outsourced and work coordinated, via telecommunications across physical locations, using customer-supplier links and teams. There are many proposals for new organizational forms that are dynamic and adaptive; network, cluster, starburst, shamrock, virtual, and spiderweb corporations all reject the hierarchical pyramid as the basis for effective organization.

Management readings: William H. Davidow and Michael S. Malone, *The Virtual Corporation* (New York: HarperBusiness, 1992); Charles Handy, *The Age of Unreason* (Boston: Harvard Business School Press, 1991).

Downsizing

Almost all process movements embrace the goal of becoming leaner. Radical transformation of the status quo is another goal of some. Radical leanness after decades of plumpness is not a matter of organizational dieting; there being no time to slim down, the surgery of downsizing is required.

Management reading: Robert M. Tamasko, *Downsizing: Reshaping the Corporation for the Future* (New York: AMACOM, 1987).

Summary

This is not an exhaustive catalog of process movements, and among those included are some that overlap. Both reengineering and total quality management emphasize the importance of teams; time-based competition, the team-based organization, and the virtual corporation share similar notions about the role of information technology as an enabler of improved business performance. But there are differences, notably (1) the primacy of radical versus sustained incremental change, (2) people versus workflow design as the starting point for planning, (3) building internal organizational capabilities versus outsourcing, and (4) technology as the key enabler of, versus support for, process change. Managers might find it useful to ask first the following questions that relate directly to these four issues and, armed with the answers, seek advice from gurus, books, consultants, and other managers.

1. What level of improvement and change are we aiming for in our business process planning—fundamental

transformation, dramatic improvement, significant improvement, or low-cost, low-effort fine-tuning? Which perspective on business processes best fits our needs and expectations?

2. Is the key to our business process change the people aspects—teams, culture, organization—or the design of the process workflows? Which of the process movements offers insights and tools most likely to get us moving?

3. Is one of our main goals to eliminate functions and enter into arrangements with other organizations, or are we more concerned with building skills and capabilities within our own organization? Which of the process movements best responds to our goals?

4. Is our planned process change primarily or secondarily reliant on computers, telecommunications, groupware, image processing, new information resources, or some other use of information technology? Which of the process movements exhibits the most sophisticated understanding of the practical issues involved in implementing information technology?

An Overview of Business Process Investment

Business Process Investment is a framework we developed to synthesize what we have learned about the focus, terms, tools, and claims of the various process movements in order to provide a comprehensive base for planning and decision making. The framework provides general classifications of types of business processes, of what we term process value builders, and of criteria for assessing process payoff, that is, the economic value of process change. Managers can use these classifications to map business process opportunities. We use them here to organize the diffuse examples across process movements of types of processes, approaches to process improvement, and measures of process benefit.

Types of business process. Viewing processes as workflows or coordination tells us something about their objectives and interfaces, but it in no way indicates their relative importance to a firm's strategic vision or contribution to its competitive position or economic performance. Business Process Investment classifies processes along two dimensions, salience and worth. Salience refers to the role of the process. Identity processes define a firm to itself, its customers, and its investors; priority processes are the engines of everyday performance; background processes are essential to operations but do not contribute directly to strategic success; mandated processes are those a firm handles because it must, regulatory compliance being an obvious example; and folklore processes are those carried on long after their useful lives are over. Worth regards the process as either an economic asset that generates value or a financial liability that drains it, where value is defined not as benefits but as the real return on invested capital generated by any benefits. The Business Process Investment framework maps processes into the Worth/Salience matrix presented in Exhibit I-1 (page 32). The matrix is the basis for targeting opportunities to create value by choosing the right process and selecting a process value builder to get the process right.

Process value builders. The aim of process change is to add value to a firm; adding value for customers often achieves this. Each of the process movements offers some insight into how to improve processes, but a comprehensive list of options has been lacking. For the Business Process Investment framework we compiled such a list (Exhibit I-2, pages 34–35). Proven approaches to process change, "process value builders," include abandon, collaborate, franchise, hub, import, invent, outsource, preempt, productize, radicalize, self-source, streamline, and worknet.

Process value metrics. Business Process Investment applies the economic value-added (EVA) framework, which measures after-tax cash flows generated by investments after deducting the cost of the capital used to create them, to measure the asset value, not just the benefits, of process improvement.

Exhibit I-1   The Worth/Salience Matrix

	WORTH	
	ASSET	LIABILITY
Identity Defines the firm to itself, its customers, and its investors		
Priority Drives everyday performance and competitive success		
Background Provides everyday operations for support of other activities		
Mandated Performed to comply with legalities and regulations		
Folklore Carried out for the sake of a rigid tradition		

SALIENCE

Business Process Investment answers questions every manager needs answered and that many of the process movements largely or entirely ignore.

1. Do we know the true economics of this process, how much of the company's capital it ties up and the cost of that capital? Nearly all of the process movements

lack an economic framework for responding to this question.

2. Is this the right process to invest our time, effort, and money in? Does our focus on workflows lead us to choose background liability processes and overlook opportunities to invest in asset processes? It is this tendency that largely accounts for the process paradox.

3. Are we assuming the solution—TQM, teams, reengineering, outsourcing—before we have examined the full range of options for building value in this process? The simultaneous strength and weakness of the individual process movements is their focused and often zealous advocacy of a clear solution to a particular problem; the danger lies in choosing a value builder before identifying the problem.

4. Are we clear about measures of payoff, not just benefits? How will benefits—time savings, cost reduction, improved service—generate economic value-added?

Answering these questions and taking appropriate action is the first step toward avoiding the process paradox.

Business Process Investment is not a challenge to the process movements, but a more systematic and comprehensive investment strategy for exploiting their insights, experience, and techniques. The Glossary defines specific terms used in process investment; these are the key ones:

Choosing the process to get right

| Background Processes | Identity Processes | Priority Processes |
| Folklore Processes | Mandated Processes | Processes as Capital |

Getting the process right

Abandon	Front-Ending	Outsource
Collaborate	Hub	Value Builders
Franchise	Import	Worknet

Exhibit I-2   Business Process Investment "Value Builders"

- Abandon: Eliminate the process (Shell Europe abandoned travel expense account reporting)

- Collaborate: Cultivate a culture and an ethos of cooperation in order to coordinate smooth and effective interactions between interdependent workers (Cemex taught its sales and production staff to work together to remove the barriers of understanding and functional priorities that impeded customer service)

- Franchise: Market a process, with supporting expertise, for someone else to turn into a business (McDonald's provided franchises with complete process capability under the McDonald's organizational brand)

- Front-end: Leave the major part of the process and supporting computer transaction processing systems as is, using computer workstations and telecommunications to add flexibility and new services at the front end and gradually erode the back end (Bell Atlantic invested $2.1 billion to front-end its customer ordering systems to provide near-immediate installation of new services)

- Hub: Bring work and information to a single customer contact point at which a process can be handled in its entirety (Mutual Benefit reduced processing time from around three weeks to two to four hours by having a case manager handle all the steps involved in issuing a new policy)

- Import: Adopt a process or process infrastructure from another industry (the State of Maryland issued benefits cards that enable holders to withdraw their welfare benefit payments from banking ATMs and to deduct food stamp usage from their accounts via credit card payment authorization terminals in supermarkets)

- Invent: Create a new process by thinking in new ways, breaking away from conceptions of an industry "core" process (Dell Computer substituted catalogs, telephone ordering, customized assembly, and UPS delivery for physical stores and inventory in the retailing of personal computers)

- Outsource: Move the process to a firm for which it is an identity asset process (Laura Ashley outsourced inventory management and distribution to FedEx)

- Preempt: Use a process infrastructure to capture another industry's traditional business at a customer moment of value (British Airways usurped international hotels' control of distribution of their own product by adding hotel reservations to its airline reservation system)

- Productize: Turn a process into a product that earns money (MCI Communications turned its own customer billing process for long-distance phone calls into a $2-billion-a-year product, "Friends and Family")

- Radicalize: Raise the salience of a process in order to accelerate the degree and pace of organizational change, transform it, or do both (Ford instituted its "Quality is Job 1" slogan)

- Self-source: Do it yourself or have the customer do it (banks installed ATMs; restaurants set up salad bars; management encouraged employees' use of laptop computers to produce their own presentation graphics and attractively formatted reports)

- Streamline: Tighten linkages between activities and eliminate waste, steps, delays, costs, and people (Toyota used lean production manufacturing processes to reduce by one-half its space requirements, investment in tools, engineering hours, and on-site inventory)

- Worknet: Provide communications infrastructures that enable individuals, groups, and outside firms to coordinate flexibly and collaboratively, and provide training, incentives, and team support for them to do so (Digital Equipment used networks as the base for worldwide, rapid building of teams for special projects and problem solving)

Understanding the underlying logic of Business
Process Investment
    Economic Value-Added   Shareholder Value
    Processes as Capital

A Word to Readers

The terms defined and assessments and examples related in the Glossary naturally reflect our authorial preferences and biases developed over long years of experience in the field. Some terms are defined briefly, others explored in greater depth. For all definitions, the goal has been to be simple, but not simplistic, and to add examples of informative and interesting analysis and discussion. A reader can use the Glossary to seek clarification or amplification of a particular term such as six sigma quality, or simply browse its pages, in which case the generous cross-referencing should be helpful. Frequent consultation should yield a solid understanding of business processes, process movements, and process investment. It is the authors' sincere hope that this book will guide its readers well on their important and challenging voyage.

Glossary

Abandon   This process value builder extends the old adage that "if a job's not worth doing, it's not worth doing well," to "if a job's not worth doing, don't do it." One of the tenets of the Business Process Reengineering movement is to rethink processes, to take a blank sheet of paper and ask, "If I were starting this company afresh, how would I design this process?" This assumes the process is needed, as most customer service processes that are the focus of reengineering and manufacturing processes that are the principal, but not exclusive, focus of total quality management are.

Candidates for abandonment are the many potential liability processes, processes that return little or no economic value-added but consume valuable capital in the form of people, facilities, computer systems, cash, and inventory. Eliminating processes is as much an investment as reengineering them. But companies must seek out such opportunities as candidate processes are not the sort that call management attention to themselves.

One European petrochemical company abandoned expense account reporting by dispensing to traveling staff with their plane tickets a per diem amount of cash, which takes into account relative hotel costs and cab fares, in the currency of the country or countries they are visiting. Staff are free to stay with friends or in inexpensive hotels and keep what money they don't spend. A

The management literature today is laden with "Re-words"— reengineer, restructure, reposition. Re- means try again. Why not just stop? If a job's not worth doing, don't do it.

cash allotment insufficient to meet expenditures for one trip is certain to be made up on another. Company cars pick staff up at their homes and meet them at the airport upon their return.

What value was created by the traditional expense reporting process, a bureaucracy that occupied office space, filing cabinets, and the time of those who had to complete travel reports and file receipts? That was capital being consumed, not just expenses being incurred. The process, even if it was the best travel expense reporting process in the world, added value to *nothing*—neither customer service nor business innovation nor quality control—relevant to the firm's market success. So why invest scarce resources in it when it can be largely eliminated?

One insurance company no longer requires that its claims adjusters submit to the full three-week review process for small claims. Solicitation of customer documents, telephone tag between adjusters and customers, and adjusters' generation of reports and filing of paperwork could drive the cost of processing above the amount of a claim.

The firm's decision to permit experienced adjusters to "eyeball" small claims—quickly review customers' histories and make judgments about whether or not to pay their claims—has enabled checks in most instances to be authorized within two days of receipt of a claim. But financial control staff were concerned that abandoning the small claims handling process, though it might improve the firm's expense ratio (i.e., the percentage of premium revenue that goes to direct expenses and overhead), would put at risk its loss ratio (i.e., the percentage of premium revenue paid out in claims, the other basic measure of an insurance firm's performance). They feared a flood of fraudulent or overstated claims that would fail to be detected owing to the elimination of management financial controls.

Their point was well taken. Citibank's reengineering of its home mortgage application and approval process had cut decision time from many weeks to fifteen minutes; customers got answers on the phone. This innovation promised to transform the mortgage lending industry, until it appeared to be busting Citibank. The streamlined process abandoned many management controls designed (like those in the insurance firm's claims handling process) to minimize risk and ensure quality loans. When it ended up with a portfolio of high-risk loans and significantly elevated default and late payment rates, Citibank abandoned the home mortgage business.

Abandoning processes or parts of processes can be an inexpensive process value builder. But care must be taken lest in abandoning a process a firm abandons controls that, however bureaucratic or performance degrading they might appear, serve a vital purpose.

Activity-Based Costing (ABC) Activity-based costing (ABC) factors in indirect costs of overhead, distribution, head office support, and so forth in order to arrive at the true costs of products and services. ABC challenges traditional allocation schemes that in no way reflect natural consumption of resources, or "level of activity."

Much of the attention being paid to business processes today is a response to the old reality of business costing having been turned on its head. For centuries, material costs and direct labor were the largest fraction of total cost in the manufacturing-based economy, with everything else lumped together as overhead. With overhead the main component of a service-dominated economy and direct labor typically accounting for less than 15 percent of product costs, how to allocate overhead, which may be thought of as *all* indirect costs, has become critically important.

By allocating overhead as a percentage of direct labor, machine hours, cost of goods, or some other direct cost, traditional cost accounting has greatly distorted the true profitability of much of American business. In a typical manufacturing environment, for example, high-volume, standard products that consume considerable labor and machine time are allocated a significant portion of the manufacturer's indirect costs, even though they con-

A company that made toilet seats sold the leftover wood. The way it allocated costs showed that it made a healthy profit on the seats and recovered some of its costs from the sale of the leftover wood. But matching costs to use of resources revealed that it lost money on toilet seats and was kept afloat by sales of the "waste" wood. Very few companies know the true cost of a process or "activity." How, then, can they make rational decisions about process investment?

sume little of the time of the quality assurance, engineering, and corporate planning departments, while many low-volume, customized products with high gross margins are made to look far less expensive to produce, market, and support than they really are. Similarly, customers who require heavy account-team time and technical support and frequently place rush orders for small lots are likely to be less profitable than those who place equivalent dollar orders for high volumes of standardized products. Traditional accounting systems do not distinguish between these two types of customer; even if the revenues they generate are the same, the profitability is not.

Assigning indirect costs on the basis of the resources consumed by specific products or services requires a detailed analysis of the relevant activities and cost structures. This can be a particularly complex task for services because they involve so few direct costs. Almost all of a service's costs are incurred in the units responsible for planning, marketing, sales, service, and support and in the many head office functions viewed as overhead.

Underlying activity-based costing is the premise that costs must be *understood* in order to be properly allocated. Consider process investment. Many of the real costs of a complex business process that spans departments, includes many and varied activities, and consumes a wide range of technical, human, and non-physical resources are unknown to or distorted by the standard accounting system. Robert Kaplan, one of ABC's main developers, suggests that activity-based costing will make inroads in companies because "It is so easy to show the inadequacies of traditional systems. The motivation to understand the cost consequences of diversity," he adds, "will be overwhelming" (Robert H. Kaplan, "Accounting for Technology Costs," *Enterprise* [Winter 1990]: 12).

Proponents of activity-based costing emphasize that nearly every standard practice in cost accounting derives from the mass production model of American business.

Whether or not activity-based costing is the answer to management's need for relevant and accurate information to help make and evaluate business process investments—and the evidence is strong in its favor—managers must be made to realize that traditional accounting systems were not devised to track end-to-end process costs. Many process costs hidden in individual departmental budgets are overlooked. The cost of services provided by the corporate legal department of a supplier of stepladders to retailers, for example, is not likely to receive much attention from a team reengineering the company's customer service process, yet it can amount to twenty-five cents of each dollar of sales! People who fall off ladders frequently blame the manufacturer and, although litigation seldom results, the legal department can devote many hours to making telephone calls, preparing letters, and conducting reviews. Perhaps the reengineering effort should consider improving customer awareness as well as streamlining the customer service process.

What is at issue here is not management accounting as such but providing accounting information for management decision making. If a customer service process consumes legal department resources, include their cost in the information provided to managers charged with improving the process.

Adhocracy   Adhocracy is one of a number of proposed new organizational forms postulated to promote flexibility, adaptability, and more timely responses to changing circumstances, capabilities deemed to be the antithesis of those fostered by bureaucracy and hierarchy. That the term is more than a little vague should hardly be surprising given that an adhocracy is, by definition, supposed to be ad hoc, to match organizational structure and strategy to the situation of the moment.

Adhocracy is most prevalent in "knowledge-based" companies such as consulting firms, research groups, specialized manufacturing, product development, and technical units. The aim of this

A fundamental challenge with which all large firms are wrestling is how to balance stability with flexibility. Stability mustn't become rigidity. Flexibility mustn't become chaos. Adhocracy pushes the extremes of flexibility to ensure rapid response to uncertain change.

organizational form is to ensure that key people are permitted to focus their talents and energy on innovation.

Innovation is key to adhocracies, the essence of and need for which are neatly captured by a leading academic.

> To innovate means to break away from established patterns. Thus, the innovative organization cannot rely on any form of standardization for coordination. It must avoid all the trappings of bureaucratic structure: sharp divisions of labor, extensive unit differentiation, highly formalized behavior, or an emphasis on planning and control systems. Above all, it must remain flexible. . . . Sophisticated innovation requires a very different configuration, one that is able to fuse experts drawn from different disciplines into smoothly functioning ad hoc teams. (Henry Mintzberg, *Mintzberg on Management: Inside Our Strange World of Organizations* [New York: Free Press, 1989].)

The characteristics of adhocracy are in many ways the ideal of most process movements. Few companies exhibit, and fewer are able to sustain, them. Adhocracies seem almost to be a transitional form and, hence, fairly unstable; the adhocratic, small, high-tech firm becomes eventually a standard business with strategic business and stable corporate R&D and finance units and numerous permanent departments. Recognizing that stability too easily becomes ossification, many firms try to temper their growth by creating small units substantially independent of the main organization. "Skunkworks" and teams assembled for a specific task or mission and disbanded upon its completion are typical approaches.

Companies with long histories of innovation are generally found to work hard to ensure that they can shift their reliance naturally and quickly between the established organization and some adhocratic component. They also exhibit the capacity to manage both and to strike a balance between innovation and stability. Widely cited examples of companies that manage adhocracy well include FedEx (via its quality action teams), Rubbermaid (perhaps the most admired company in America owing largely to its cross-functional product development teams), Intel (the pace-setter and dominant force in the global computer chip market still), and Motorola (through the agency of its quality teams).

Adhocracy is a response to change as the norm. It may also be a necessary precondition for managing the radical change proposed by so many of the process movements.

Agency Theory   Agency theory is concerned with how parties involved in an economic agreement or relationship can be motivated to act in their joint, rather than their respective self, interest. It addresses a key issue for process improvement that relies on cooperation and teamwork: what is the basis for mutual trust?

Treated primarily in esoteric academic economic journals, and hence unfamiliar to most managers, agency theory exerted a strong influence on research into business strategy. More important for our purposes, it addresses a practical and often neglected issue that is central to process change: the design of incentive agreements for individuals and groups that bring conflicting interests or priorities to a shared activity. Such incentives assume added importance in the face of the growing trend to outsource processes and even entire functions, enter into cooperative alliances, and employ electronic links to directly connect with customers. Whatever the intended degree of cooperation, each party must protect its own interests.

Agency theory defines contractual incentives, information needed for management oversight and control, and decision rights that enable each party to protect its interests, but not at the expense of other parties. It also addresses what is termed the principal/agent element of manager/employee relationships. It assumes that, all else being equal, the agent wants to shirk. Employees slack off, suppliers cheat, managers try to manipulate capital budgeting and performance reporting systems, and executives strive to maximize their earnings and perquisites at the expense of workers and shareholders.

Like much of traditional economics, agency theory assumes

Companies easily talk about being "partners" with their customers and suppliers. With the best will in the world, they still have conflicting interests. How can these be resolved and all protect their interests while preserving trust? Agency theory provides the esoteric answers. The question it raises is fundamental to outsourcing, supply chain management, joint ventures, and even manager-employee relationships and "empowerment."

complete selfishness, does not admit culture, affiliation, equity, values, or sense of participation as modifiers thereof. But it does deal with some practical issues often ignored by process movements, among them: (1) what incentives powerful customers might offer suppliers to offset their costs of complying with requirements to use electronic data interchange to process purchase orders, shorten delivery times, and improve component quality; (2) what might constitute motivators and rewards for groups of employees asked to participate in plans to radically redesign processes or downsize, which is to say, help eliminate many of their own jobs; (3) the incongruity of massive cost-cutting programs launched, or employee wage cuts or freezes imposed, by top management teams that reward themselves with huge bonuses and salary increases.

Issues of incentives, rewards, and risk sharing are largely ignored in the mainstream literature on the process movements. Frequently, imbalance of power is all the incentive that is needed. The incentive many large firms proffer to suppliers required to accommodate electronic data interchange is preservation of their contracts; the comparable incentive for employees asked to participate in radical restructuring is the chance that they might keep their jobs.

Unfortunately, agency theory tends to be an exercise in mathematics, make simplifying assumptions about the nature of business and organization, and be communicated in mind-numbing prose. It is an analytic framework rather than a practical tool. Its value is in the questions it raises, not the answers it provides. The questions are ones every manager needs to ask.

- Who is the principal here—the person, group, or business that constitutes the "customer" or initiator of the proposed process change—and who is the agent charged with bringing about the change?

- What power does each exert over the other? Is the balance of power, benefits, and costs fair?

- Can the parties involved be made to act in their own interests in a way that yields mutual benefits?

- What contractual arrangements (corporate equivalents of prenuptial agreements) might be needed?

- What incentives must be offered?

- What information do the participating parties need to monitor progress and performance?

Many joint ventures, alliances, and outsourcing projects have failed because these questions were not asked. Cooperation, partnership, and teamwork require mutual trust. Agency theory views trust in terms of formal contracts and monitoring mechanisms. Its philosophy is aptly summed up by President Reagan's comment on nuclear disarmament: "Trust—but verify."

Agile Manufacturing Agile manufacturing is a recent movement viewed by the auto industry, which shares with the consumer electronics industry the distinction of being the pacesetter in manufacturing process innovation, as the next step in its development. It represents the demise of the century-long tradition of manufacturing driven by scale. It aspires to total flexibility without sacrificing quality or incurring added costs.

Agile manufacturing is contrasted with lean production, Toyota's composite of tools, culture, and organizational philosophy that ensures high quality, low cost, and continuous and sustained improvement. The Japanese Manufacturing 21 (twenty-first century) consortium defines it in terms of nine major challenges to car makers, one being the three-day car, three days from customer order for a customized car to dealer delivery. The goal is practical; leading Japanese auto makers can deliver the ten-day car now.

U.S. firms moving in the same direction have a strong advantage over Japanese companies in some areas relevant to the nine challenges of Manufacturing 21.

1. Break dependency on scale and economies of scale (reducing setup costs is key).

Japanese companies invented just-in-time manufacturing, lean production, flexible manufacturing, and many of the tools of total quality management. Even as the rest of the world catches up and some companies overtake them, they are positioning for the next leap forward. So, too, are their American competitors. The three-day car is coming. Flexible manufacturing is adaptive; agile production is adaptive and faster. The aim of lean manufacturing is to keep production steady and predictable and minimize cost and waste in a world of business that is increasingly unpredictable and unsteady.

2. Produce vehicles in low volumes at reasonable cost (Nissan's Intelligent Body System, a Lego-block approach that favors existing over newly designed body components, leaves tooling as the only major expense for a new model).

3. Guarantee the three-day car.

4. Replace large centralized with distributed clusters of mini-assembly plants located near customers (as much as five days' time is required to ship cars to dealers; Japan's horrendous traffic congestion has become the weak link in just-in-time inventory management, with suppliers unable to deliver on time).

5. Be able to reconfigure components in many different ways.

6. Make work stimulating (those who carry out Lego-block production should not be treated as Lego blocks).

7. Turn the customer into a "prosumer," an ugly neologism that means proactive something; the idea is that the customer will take an active role in the product design by, for example, configuring options at a computer in a dealer showroom.

8. Streamline ordering systems and establish close relationships with suppliers.

9. Manage the massive volumes of data generated by the production system so as to be able to analyze that data quickly and agilely.

Agile production would appear to be the blueprint for future manufacturing. Managers in every industry would do well to incorporate the essence of the Manufacturing 21 challenges into their agendas. Publishing, retailing, and banking are but a few of the industries likely to rally around agility.

Alliances   *See* Partnerships and Alliances

Background Processes In the Business Process Investment framework, necessary elements of everyday operations such as payroll and accounts payable processes and the mass of administrative workflows that characterize most companies' operations are termed background processes. They are contrasted with identity processes that define a business to itself, its customers, and its investors, that make a company "different" or "special," and priority processes that drive daily business performance and, thus, exert a strong influence on a firm's competitive positioning and growth.

The background label should be applied judiciously. What is background for one business may well be in the foreground for another. Distribution may be a background process for a pharmaceutical company but a priority process for a retailer; yet for Dell Computer and Lands' End, it is an identity process. Identity and priority processes relate directly to a firm's strategic vision and competitive strengths. Because background processes generally do not, they represent, by and large, financial liabilities. They consume capital without generating value. Take payroll. Can you imagine the CEO of any company sending a message to the staff announcing a bonus and special celebration because "This week we had the best payroll process we've had in our entire history—it was great!" Obviously not. Payroll is a background process. It is important that it be handled well and that any opportunity to cut costs and improve quality (i.e., reliability and accuracy) be examined. But even were quality to be improved by a factor of two, the process improvement, unlike improvements in priority and identity processes, would not add value, though it might reduce costs.

A review of published accounts of business process reengineering projects will reveal a disproportionate number of background liability processes among the targets. There are four clear reasons for this.

1. Background, especially administrative and customer support processes, embody many of the organizational

It is not at all surprising that reengineering's early promise has been followed by frequently disappointing results. If it is targeted to business processes that do not directly relate to the identity asset processes that establish a firm's competitive differentiation or to the priority processes that drive its everyday competitive performance, even dramatic improvements will have little impact on overall success. Background processes are part of everyday business but do not directly generate economic value-added for a firm. Reengineering payroll, however brilliantly you do it, will not turn your firm into a competitive superstar.

ailments the reengineering movement seeks to redress, namely: functional division of labor; many departments, steps, and delays; complex controls and supervisory mechanisms; too much paper; and fiefdoms and "bureaucracy."

2. Workflows are clearly identifiable and inputs (customer requests) and outputs (documents, loans, transactions) well defined, making such processes easy to conceptualize and model.

3. Information technology has been used to automate, and often bureaucratize, the processes or been little used at all, leaving opportunities to exploit telecommunications, information, and customer service workstations to dramatically simplify, speed up, and streamline sequences of workflows and decision making.

4. Because they are part of "internal" operations and have evolved over many years to meet internal organizational needs, expectations, budgets, and structures, background processes are almost invariably designed with limited attention to customer needs.

Although a natural focus for the industrial engineering approaches of reengineering and total quality management, turning background liability processes in background asset processes by cutting costs and thereby freeing up capital can consume substantial resources and involve complex organizational change and yield only limited results. They may be obvious, yet not be the right processes to get right. Consider the classic case of Mutual Benefit. Its success at cutting the insurance policy issuing process from weeks to hours was widely publicized in an article that, in effect, launched the reengineering movement, yet the firm flirted with bankruptcy and was taken over by state insurance regulators. Why? Because it had neglected priority liability processes for managing both its investment portfolio and relationships with customers, investors, and regulators. The reengineering achievement broke new ground and was a striking success, but, because it was accomplished for a background process, it could not yield benefits sufficient to offset the company's other process liabilities.

Background liability processes do waste resources and engender complexity and bureaucracy, but they can be addressed by other value builders than reengineering. A useful principle for Process Investment is to outsource background liability processes to firms for which they are identity asset processes. Payroll, a background liability process for the typical firm, is the identity asset process for ADP, the company that processes roughly half of all U.S. payroll transactions. Similarly, tax reporting and accounting are background liability processes for British Petroleum but identity asset processes for the Big Six accounting firms. Outsourcing guided by this proviso is generally a win-win situation.

Baldrige Award The most prestigious quality award in the United States, the Baldrige Award is administered by the National Institute of Standards and Technology, an agency of the U.S. Department of Commerce, and the American Society for Quality Control. It is funded and managed by private sector organizations and draws on many sources for the examiners who conduct exhaustive reviews of applicants. As many as six winners are selected annually, with up to two winners in each of three categories: manufacturing, service, and small business.

The many firms, small and large, that invest substantial financial and organizational resources in efforts to win the Baldrige Award often find that even when they do not succeed, the application process is sufficiently rigorous to force valuable, fundamental reevaluations of manufacturing and service processes. The award emphasizes specific core values and concepts that add up to a quality-driven business strategy.

- Customer-driven quality—ongoing support and relationships, efforts to retain existing and attract new customers, speed of response, and other service

The Baldrige Award is as much a discipline as a prize. Its categories and criteria have provided many companies opportunities for often disturbing self-diagnosis; what is perceived to be good shape turns out, by the standards of Baldrige winners, to have been self-deception. Just applying for the Baldrige can push a firm to new levels of quality. IBM's Rochester plant, recognizing it as an opportunity for learning and improvement, repeated the entire application process the year after it won the Baldrige, even though the award is never presented two years in a row to the same group.

characteristics must be viewed from the customer's perspective.

- Leadership—top management must be a role model in its commitment to quality by demonstrating, not just demanding, a customer focus.

- Continuous improvement—not a limited, compartmentalized program, but an integral part of work activities across the firm.

- Employee participation and development—elements include education, morale, rewards, empowerment, safety, and dedication.

- Fast response—*the* basic requirement for service, adaptability, and product and market initiatives.

- Design quality and problem prevention—a basic tenet of the total quality movement is that it is far less costly to prevent defects at the design stage and catch problems early by building quality into the design of and processes associated with products and services than to try to inspect them out at the end of manufacturing, distribution, or service processes.

- Long-range outlook—momentum is sustained by a willingness to make long-term investments and commitments.

- Management by fact—quality assessment and improvement are based on collection, analysis, and use of customer data, benchmarking against other companies, reliable performance measures, employee feedback, supplier information, and so forth; management by fact emphasizes objectivity over opinion, information over guesswork, and accountability over "that's not my job."

- Partnership development—targets include suppliers, customers, employees and unions, and research and educational institutions.

- Corporate responsibility and citizenship—ethics, protection of the environment, conservation, safety, and community responsibility are legitimate business links to the broader society.

Reviewers score firms on seven categories developed around these core values and concepts. The distribution of 1,000 total points is adjusted annually; as of 1994, it was:

- leadership, 90 points;
- information and analysis, 80 points;
- strategic quality planning, 60 points;
- human resource development and management, 150 points;
- management of process quality, 140 points;
- quality and operational results, 180 points;
- customer focus and satisfaction, 300 points.

The model for the Baldrige Award was the Japanese Deming Prize (named for Dr. W. E. Deming, a founding father of the total quality management movement). The aggressive pursuit of the Deming Prize by Japanese manufacturers has been deemed a major contributor to elevating Japanese manufacturing quality far above that of most American firms by the late 1980s. Many years of planning and lobbying were required to spur Congress to pass legislation (in 1987) enabling a comparable U.S. award that might be a rallying point for quality efforts, highlight the best of American business, and advance new standards for emulation. The award was named posthumously for the late U.S. Secretary of Commerce Malcolm Baldrige.

Applying for the Baldrige is expensive. The requisite operational analyses and remediation of weaknesses may necessitate the launch of organizational change programs. Many firms have publicly acknowledged the immense value of a forced, floor-to-ceiling, in-depth review guided by the tough Baldrige criteria and standards. IBM's Rochester plant, having won the award in 1990, was ineligible for it in 1991, yet went through the entire process of filling out an application on the chance that it might identify further "holes" in its operations. A number of large manufacturers require that their suppliers undergo the application process for the same reason. Indeed, a mini-industry has grown up around the award that includes education programs, cooperative forums for inter-company benchmarking, and quality consultants (including consultants who know how to win the award).

The review process is also expensive, complex, and time consuming. More than 250 expert examiners drawn from a wide range of backgrounds and organizations first score written applications to provide a basis for selecting companies that warrant in-depth site visits.

Winners of the Baldrige Award have included many paragons of American business that have made "quality" a watchword and built a powerful combination of culture, strategy, technology, and process. FedEx and Motorola are distinctive examples. Others, somewhat less exemplary, highlight the process paradox: that great success in process improvement may not translate into business success. IBM and General Motors both garnered the award at the very time their competitive position, management leadership, and production innovation were faltering. One small firm that took the award expended so much time, money, and effort at the expense of doing business that it was forced to file for bankruptcy only a year later.

Critics of the Baldrige Award variously point to its relatively narrow conception of quality, application costs that can discourage or ruin medium-sized and small applicants, and the gamesmanship many firms employ, including the retention of former reviewers as consultants. Award criteria and categories are continuously revised to address these complaints, and all in all the Baldrige is widely respected.

The Baldrige Award has provided a focus for the increasingly successful efforts of U.S. businesses to catch up with their Japanese rivals, for service organizations to embrace the total quality management focus that was heretofore largely confined to manu-facturing, and for widespread diffusion of the terms and concepts of the quality movement.

Benchmarking   Benchmarking is the calibration of your firm's performance with that of another that represents the best in the field. Historically, U.S. firms have tended to look inward rather than outward, to be secretive about their operations and take a parochial view of their competitive arenas, closely attending to their traditional competition but largely ignoring companies in other industries. The problems of the U.S. auto industry in the 1970s and 1980s, the fall from grace and growth of IBM and General Motors, and the frequency with which domestic compa-nies underestimated the growing capacity of foreign competitors and new industry entrants were rooted in a combination of intro-version, secrecy, and parochialism. Too many U.S. firms have suffered from the "not invented here" syndrome; if it wasn't invented here, we don't need to know about it.

Benchmarking takes firms in the opposite direction, to learn from those that are the best. Fundamentally a matter of humility, it played a major role in Xerox's quality management-engineered turnaround in the early 1980s. Indeed, the term was popularized by Xerox at a time when, not coincidentally, the company had fallen badly behind its competitors, to the extent that Canon was able to make a better product than Xerox and sell it for less than Xerox's *manufacturing* cost. Xerox had to learn and learn fast. It learned about order processing by benchmarking itself against mail order retailer L.L. Bean.

A health care insurance company that had targeted customer service processes for benchmarking identified firms, including Xerox and L.L. Bean, that stood out for service. Benchmark can-didates must have been finalists for or winners of the Baldrige Award, guaranteed levels of service to customers (e.g., "same-day shipping," "your money back if . . ."), and provided "one-stop" shopping by telephone (specifically, to complete a transaction

How does our firm compare with XYZ? If XYZ is just the rest of our industry or our main competitors, benchmarking against them is likely to provide limited insight and payoff. When XYZ is the best of the best, there's plenty to learn and apply. When Southwest Airlines, the best of the best in airline processes, wanted to improve the cleaning and refuelling of its planes and turn them around quickly, it benchmarked its performance against that of Indy 500 pit crews.

must have required no more than a single call to one service agent). The process was conducted by a cross-functional team that assessed, among other performance measures, absentee rates of customer service staff, training time, call volumes per service agent, percentage of callers left on hold who eventually hung up, percentage of calls that resulted in callback, and turnover rates. Information gleaned from the benchmarking process was used to guide a redesign of the company's customer service processes. Job functions were changed to accommodate team servicing; physical layouts and furnishings were altered to improve efficiency; additional training was implemented; and new customer information systems were inaugurated and telecommunications facilities installed. The results were striking; in some instances, a 100 percent performance improvement was realized.

The foregoing example illustrates some key criteria for successful benchmarking.

- *Know your own operations.* To know what to benchmark, a firm must know its strengths and weaknesses. The health care firm spent a considerable amount of time choosing relevant performance measures.

- *Focus on the details.* Benchmarking isn't a matter of visiting, say, L.L. Bean to see how it handles customer calls. It's more a matter of posing a difficult question, for example: "L.L. Bean has 48 percent less turnover than we do. Why?"

- *Find the best of the best.* Locating the best requires a broad awareness of business trends outside, as well as within, an industry. In the absence of a suitable company, use criteria for success in the Baldrige Award program.

- Use benchmarks to monitor progress during and after implementation. Benchmark-derived measures are literally process performance metrics and are ideally made part of ongoing management and staff feedback, analysis, and response.

A significant and growing problem in benchmarking is getting access to the best of the best. The attention accorded, and their justifiable pride in, their operations notwithstanding, firms such as L.L. Bean cannot be expected to affably host an interminable stream of visitors who would be emulators.

For virtually every quality management-related concept there is a Japanese word. For benchmarking, it is *dantotsu,* which means striving to be the "best of the best." Benchmarking begins by identifying, and ends by rigorously and systematically trying to unseat, the best of the best.

See also Best Practice

Benefits of Process Improvements Benefits are the qualitative and quantitative measures of improvement in a process. They are indicators of progress. They are not necessarily measures of payoff. Payoff is an economic concept, benefits an operational management measure. Some benefits translate directly into economic value-added; that is, they generate positive after-tax cash flows after the cost of the capital consumed in adding value to the processes is subtracted.

It is vital that managers not equate benefits with value/payoff. A deliberately silly example illustrates why. Consider a process improvement project that provides immense benefits and greatly improves customer service and satisfaction. Costs are slashed by 75 percent. Staff savings in time average 35 percent. The investment is small, a few thousand dollars. Errors are almost entirely eliminated. This is obviously a great business deal, well worth writing up in an article for a leading business publication such as the *Harvard Business Review,* until it is learned that the process improvement is to replace the head office's cafeteria with self-service coffee machines. The benefits are real, but the impact on business performance is trivial (unless, of course, a direct correlation can be established between caffeine and productivity). If the example was self-service diagnosis of medical symptoms and scheduling of patient appointments (an innovation first intro-

Benefits are not necessarily value. That said, it is now routine to realize benefits of 40 percent in terms of quality improvement, time, cost, and error reduction. Aiming for 20 percent is just tinkering. Choose the process for which the 40 percent translates directly to business value.

duced by the Harvard Community Health Plan) or self-service devices for creating customized music tapes on retailers' premises, perhaps the article is on again.

The point is that benefits tell one nothing about value-added. Consider another, more practical and very typical example that demonstrates that you can't determine the value of benefits if you can't establish the cost of generating them. The process improvement directly affects customer service in key areas and cuts costs by $3 million as part of a downsizing program that sees 350 staff laid off in the head office. The total cost of the project, including the computer and communications systems that streamline the process, reduce staffing requirements, and speed response to customers, is $2 million. Revenues increase by an estimated 10 percent.

A great deal? Maybe. But only if all process capital costs are fully accounted for. What about the 350 staff laid off? If their offices remain vacant in a building leased by the company, the rental cost isn't eliminated. What about the $2 million investment cost? If, say, $1 million was for information systems development, the true capital cost for the next five years is at least $5 million. This is because every dollar spent on development directly generates 40 cents of operations costs and 20 cents of ongoing maintenance costs (repairing the inevitable "bugs" that are intrinsic to complex software systems and adapting the system to new requirements; when, for example, federal tax law changes, it is not an option to say, "We prefer to abide by the old laws that are compatible with our systems."). By the same token, $400,000 allocated for personal computers would represent a small capital investment compared against the $3 million in cost savings, until the costs of supporting a $5,000 personal computer, estimated by reliable sources to be between $8,000 and $18,000 per year, are taken into account. Add to the $400,000 a capital commitment of between $3.2 million and $7.2 million, the costs of severance for the 350 laid-off staff, inevitable future training costs, and the cost of management time consumed by the process improvement project and it is not at all clear that the aggregate benefits yield real economic value-added.

The process movements largely lack a systematic and reliable economic model. They assume too readily that benefits translate to value-added and largely underestimate life-cycling process costs. That's why McKinsey's study of business process reengineering "successes" discussed in the Introduction concludes that "companies achieve dramatic improvements in individual processes only to watch overall results decline."

Of course, if there are no benefits there can be no value and firms must target specific operational benefits in order to create value. Benefit measures are the performance metrics used to target opportunities, plan the implementation of process changes, and monitor progress. Very roughly, benefits from process change take the form either of (1) improvements in process outputs such as quality, service, and customer satisfaction, or (2) time improvements in process execution. If there is one single and universal measure of process improvement benefits, it is time. Time is the relevant measure when numbers of steps and staff involved in a process are reduced, when improvements are realized in responsiveness and service to customers, when organizational levels are eliminated, activities streamlined, and so forth. "Productivity," however defined and measured, is in essence a matter of return on time.

Ensuring the link between benefits and economic value is increasingly the single most important issue in process investment. It is also the weakest element in the process movements taken together and the potential Achilles heel of the business process reengineering movement in particular.

Best Practice Companies increasingly recognize that comparing themselves to their existing competition can lead to complacency and overlooked opportunities. Say your firm's claims handling process averages fifteen days versus the industry average of twenty-six. So? You've reduced claims processing errors from 13

Locating best practice means thinking outside the bounds of traditional industry and established competition. When a leading personal computer manufacturer looked at best practice in packing small orders compactly and in a way that would prevent damage in transit, it zeroed in on Marriott's unit that supplies airline meals—including lettuce, cutlery, and accompanying taste-free polystyrofeed—packed so that the contents do not wilt, spill, or leak. The manufacturer ended up outsourcing its small-order fulfillment to Marriott, whose best practice it could never match.

percent to 3 percent in five years. The comparison tells you nothing.

Best practice is what has been achieved by the industry leader and is thus achievable by others. Increasingly, firms committed to radical improvement in their business processes seek out best practice and set attainable, if ambitious, targets. Almost always, a firm finds best practice outside its industry. Xerox, for example, found best practice in orders fulfillment in mail order retailer L.L. Bean. Xerox could learn more about order fulfillment from Bean than from another photocopier maker. Similarly, Southwest Airlines, today's process leader in the U.S. airline industry, looked to pit crews at the Indianapolis 500 raceway for best practice in between-flight refuelling and servicing of aircraft.

Many companies, particularly multinationals, are looking internally for best practices with the aim of transferring the sucess of the business groups that have effectively reengineered processes and, often, the team responsible for the reengineering effort elsewhere in the company.

Variants of best practice are "best in breed," "best in class," "best in the world," and "best of the best" (the Japanese equivalent of "best practice"). You get the message: good isn't good enough today.

Best practice and benchmarking are closely related and the terms are often used interchangeably.

See also Benchmarking

BPR   *See* Business Process Reengineering

Most definitions take a narrow view of business processes as distinct flows of work, a limiting perspective that can divert attention and resources.

Business Process   The many definitions of business process, most of which focus on workflows, are summarized, and their implications for management action discussed, in the Introduction.

Business Process Reengineering   It was the reengineering movement that brought the term "business process" into the mainstream of management and made both process and reengineering part of everyday thinking and vocabulary. This gave rise to so many different approaches and consulting methodologies that today it is difficult to get a clear picture of just what reengineering really is.

Reengineering is less a set of formal tools and techniques than an attitude toward change. Whereas the total quality management movement emphasizes transformation through sustained continuous improvement, the ethos of reengineering is radical and dramatic change. Reengineering presumes that most processes aren't working anywhere near as well as they should and that a committed and urgent effort is needed to transform them. One reason reengineering took off in the early 1990s is that it provided managers with a vocabulary and, to some extent, justification for mobilizing the organization for basic change. It defined change in terms not of "strategy," "marketing," and "customer service" but of "roll up your sleeves, folks, and get moving fast." It represented an alternative to a decade of continuous struggling to cope with ever more potent forces of change. Reengineering was in many ways a response to the waste and productivity crisis in large organizations, which may explain why it took off so dramatically and quickly.

Michael Hammer and James Champy articulate a set of principles for the reengineering movement, define four roles essential for implementation, and characterize the results of a successful program. These principles are obviously ideals; they require transformation of just about every functional element in the organization. Moreover, although reengineering espouses worker empowerment, managers as coaches, and many of the features of the team-based, networked organization, its radicalism and conception of business processes primarily as workflows often engenders a contradiction between principles and practice. Reengineering is very much top-down driven and committed to radical, read ruthless, change, to the extent that more and more articles on the subject equate reengineering with layoffs. It is difficult to "empower" teams of workers to fire themselves.

Much of U.S. car makers' success in improving manufacturing quality and cutting costs was wasted through inattention to management succession, acquisition, board governance, labor relations, and executive promotion processes. Investing in these would have saved a number of firms literally billions of dollars and quite probably close to a million jobs. It's these "soft" processes that explain most of the relative successes and failures in the histories of Ford, Honda, Toyota, Penske, Volvo, Ford, VW, and General Motors.

Touted as the breakthrough in business transformation, reengineering has subsequently transformed itself into ill-advised cost cutting and eliminating peoples' jobs.

Fundamentally, reengineering is an ethos of change: it elevates radical change over traditional, phased, sustained incremental improvement. The popularity of reengineering largely reflects crisis in most large organizations— waste, overstaffing, eroding margins, and unacceptable productivity growth. Reengineering is aimed at jump-starting the stalled corporation. That's the "why" of reengineering. Some exponents argue that the why demands a brutal "how."

Principles of Reengineering

- Combine several jobs into one; don't view processes in departmental terms; use information technology to move and process paper; rethink the roles of the people who provide customer service and try to build the process from the customer contact point back instead of from the head office forward.

- Allow workers to make decisions; customer service agents should never have to say, "I'm sorry, I need to get authorization for this," or "Our standard agreement is ———," or "Yes, I understand your point but ———."

- Perform process steps in a natural order; begin with the customer and work back; begin dialogues with "How can I help you," not "Before you fill out the application form we need a copy of your tax return." Avoid frustrating customers with processes that don't make sense to them.

- Recognize that processes have multiple versions; flexibility is the norm, rigid standardization the exception, a reversal of the historical design of operations.

- Perform work where it makes most sense; telecommunications is rendering more and more work location-independent.

- Reduce checks and controls; minimize the influence of bureaucracy and "the green eye shade crew" (accountants and financial controllers).

- Minimize reconciliation; get the work done and look after reporting later.

- Provide a single point of contact in a case manager.

- Emphasize hybrid centralized/decentralized operations; eliminate the dichotomy between centralization and decentralization by using telecommunications to support central management, but decentralized use of inventory, for example.

Four Roles in Reengineering Implementation

- The process leader, a senior executive, authorizes and motivates the overall effort.
- The process owner has responsibility for both the existing process and the reengineering program.
- The reengineering team diagnoses the process and oversees its redesign and subsequent reimplementation.
- The steering committee oversees the organization's overall reengineering strategy and sets policy guidelines.

Typical Results of a Successful Reengineering Program

- Work units shift from functional departments to process teams.
- Job tasks change from simple to multidimensional.
- People's roles shift from controlled to empowered.
- Job preparation migrates from training to education.
- The focus of performance measures and compensation shifts from activity to results.
- Performance gives way to ability as an advancement criterion.
- Values shift from protective to productive.
- Managers leave off supervising and begin to coach.
- Hierarchical organizational structures are flattened.
- Executive responsibility shifts from scorekeeping to leading.

Source: Adapted from Michael Hammer and James Champy, *Reengineering the Corporation: A Manifesto for Business Revolution* (New York: HarperBusiness, 1993), ch. 3, p. 102, and ch. 4, respectively.

Case Manager A case manager is a single point of contact for customers, an individual who is authorized to process a transaction from start to finish. The term, coined by advocates of business process reengineering, characterizes an important aspect of that movement's interpretation of customer service. The new take on customer service, easily the most frequent achievement of business process reengineering, is exemplified by insurance industry leader USAA. Telephone calls to USAA's toll-free customer service number are routed to computer workstation–based agents who are able to retrieve instantly the requisite information and authorized to process in their entirety transactions ranging from answering questions about coverage, to changing policy information, to making an automobile loan.

The customer service agent who answers your call to the insurance firm USAA can access all the information the firm has about you, including electronic copies of handwritten letters. The agent can process your entire "case" and not submit you to the time-wasting, "Sorry, you need to phone. . . ." Most successful redesign of customer service processes relies on bringing work and information to a case manager in this way and making fifteen minutes the time to handle transactions that used to take days or even weeks.

The concept of case management may well be process innovation/redesign/reengineering's single most important contribution to business. It substitutes integration for division of labor, the norm in organizations for more than a century. Division of labor breaks complex tasks into component tasks that can be handled by staff with specialized skills and focused responsibilities. Thus, the purchasing department orders goods and accounts receivable authorizes, and finance makes, payment. At the extreme of division of labor we have the automobile assembly line, on which individual workers exert little or no influence over and exhibit negligible knowledge of and, in many instances, interest in any but their own circumscribed process activities.

Proponents of reengineering emphasize that division of labor is antithetical to the process view. From the process perspective, a process is a single job, not the series of separate "jobs" into which division of labor disaggregates it. Reengineering assigns responsibility for that process to a single individual, the case manager. The impact of case management on process execution can be dramatic. IBM Credit Corporation's process for issuing computer financing quotes used to require seven days and span five functional areas. Today it is handled by a case manager and takes six hours. Structuring the job around the process flow rather than the reverse has enabled IBM to prepare ten times as many quotes as it did ten years ago with fewer staff than it had then. Or consider the installation of Centrex telephone service, which took Pacific Bell five days and involved eleven jobs and the updating of nine computer systems. Not surprisingly, errors and rework were frequent and representatives often had to return to customers for additional information, which introduced delays and engendered frustration. Today, with service coordinators handling all customer contacts and directly interacting with all computer systems from their computer workstations, 80 percent of orders can be filled on the same day. In both companies, the customer now has a single point of contact, the case manager.

Case management is becoming common in customer service. Its features are standard across types of business and service.

- A case manager (an individual or part of a team of case managers who share the workload) handles a process end to end, from the making to the fulfillment of a customer request.

- Customers have a single point of contact, the case manager, usually reached through a toll-free telephone number.

- Case managers enjoy considerable discretion in dealing with problems and exceptions; empowerment is essential for case managers who are expected to provide real service, not just execute rote steps in a process.

- Work and information flow to and from case managers, who are, in effect, centers of hubs; they do not have to send paper to another department for, say, placing an order but instead update the relevant computer systems directly from the workstation. Similarly, the case managers never have to say, "I don't know; you need to contact our XYZ department to get an answer to your question." The XYZ department is in effect in the computer workstation.

Massive organizational change is implicit in a shift from the traditional organization of work along functional and departmental lines to integration of work across an entire process. Case management may be far more rewarding, but it is also generally more demanding and stressful. It requires new personal skills, end-to-end process knowledge, and familiarity with often complex computer systems. Moreover, the work can be isolating, involving limited interaction with other workers and demanding intense concentration. At the extreme, it creates a sort of service factory, with case managers no less chained to their telephones or service desks than auto workers to their assembly line stations. Finally, it is all too tempting for managers to monitor worker productivity via computer, using detailed performance reporting to measure even the average length of customer telephone calls.

On the positive side, case management almost invariably improves customer satisfaction and reduces both company costs and service delivery time, often dramatically. Fifteen minutes is the new norm for service at the customer moment of value when case management is combined with information technology.

Its negative side is summarized in an article on case management.

> [People] feel they are not doing their jobs if they are not peering at the screen, typing at the keyboard, or talking on the telephone. Even when the job involves analyzing real customer problems or talking to real customers on the telephone, tangible social interaction is lost. Even the tangibility of paper and files is missed; as one case manager put it, "Instead of putting a completed file into the out-box, I feel like I am sending it into a black hole." (Thomas H. Davenport and Nitin Nohria, "Case Management and the Division of Labor," *Sloan Management Review* [winter 1994]: 19.)

Many firms address the negatives by employing case management teams, often, ironically, reintroducing division of labor into the process.

Firms committed to reengineering customer service processes are clearly moving toward case management. The significant organizational challenges they will almost surely encounter on this route are often underestimated by proponents of reengineering who adopt an industrial engineering perspective on workflows. Not mentioned in the articles and books lauding one of the first and most successful instances of case management, the Mutual Benefit insurance company, is that the stresses, uncertainties, and difficulties of learning new skills led some employees to express their frustration by picketing their employer's head office.

Cause-and-Effect Diagrams   Also known as fishbone charts (after their appearance) or Ishikawa diagrams (after their Japanese inventor), cause-and-effect diagrams are widely used in total quality management to identify all possible causes of a problem. The problem-solving team writes a brief description of the problem (the "effect") on the right side of the diagram (see below); brainstorming possible causes, which are usually categorized as manpower, machines, methods, and materials, yields the bones of the "fish."

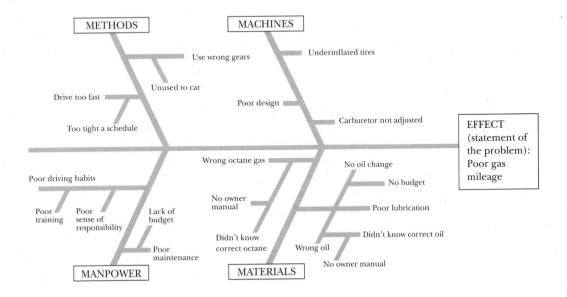

The goal is to cure the cause, not list the symptoms.

Cause-and-effect diagrams encourage a disciplined approach to problem resolution. Often, they are employed as part of a six-step process.

1. Agree on a statement of the problem.

2. Generate, through data collection, brainstorming, or both, a list of possible causes.

3. Sort the list by category and ask, "Why does this happen?"

4. Look for patterns and repetition that might identify the most basic causes.

5. Verify relationships between causes and effects.

6. Remedy the causes.

Underlying Ishikawa's method is the assumption that a problem will have more than one cause.

Cell Manufacturing Cell manufacturing is the technique of using small teams of workers to produce a complete product. Typically, a cell consists of a team of five to fifty people physically grouped around all the manufacturing equipment they need. The cell makes the entire product, checks it, and may even package it, taking full responsibility for meeting quality and customer requirements.

Cell manufacturing directly challenges the logic of mass production and is a manifestation of the growing emphasis on team-based operations. It is also a response to the need for what is termed "mass customization": tailoring the manufacturing of a "standard" product to the customer's special needs. While changing a production line to add features, permit variety, or handle very small lot sizes is costly in time and money, cells can make such modifications on the fly. Moreover, since the cell works item by item to produce finished goods, far less inventory is in process at any point.

The first cars were built to order. Henry Ford's Model T assembly line, however, kicked off an era of mass production that may only now be drawing to a close. With consumers once again valuing variety, cell manufacturing is returning to the old "craft" production to provide what they want. Cell manufacturing works best for products that are relatively labor intensive in use of machinery and that share common components. Though it increases training needs by an estimated 50 percent, the payoff is speed and flexibility.

Harley-Davidson illustrates the success of cells, which have been used in firms like Toyota, Sony, and Mazda for many years but which have come more recently to American firms. The 900 manufacturing workers in Harley's engine and gearbox plant produce parts such as cylinder heads. Formerly, it took a week to make these parts, and parts might sit in boxes as they worked their way through the manufacturing process. Now that the parts are built by two-person cells, manufacturing time has been reduced to no more than three hours, inventory has been reduced because sudden spurts in demand have been eliminated, floor space has been reduced by 30 percent, and inventory turns over fourteen times a year as compared with four and a half times ten years ago.

Compaq's fight back against Dell and manufacturers of PC "clones" in the early 1990s relied partly on shifting from assembly lines to cells—and productivity grew by around 25 percent. (The figure is comparable for Lexmark, the maker of computer printers that was originally part of IBM and bought out by a group of employees.) Compaq's goal is to build all its computers to the exact specifications of customers and retailers. The cell, not the assembly line, is the natural way of organizing to meet this goal.

Client/Server Computing   Client/server computing combines four building blocks of computers and telecommunications:

1. tools, primarily personal computers and telephones, for accessing information and services;

2. telecommunications links to remote services;

3. information stores, primarily data bases;

4. transaction processing engines, complex assemblies of powerful hardware and software.

Information stores and transaction processing services have traditionally been managed by large "mainframe" computers. Limited functionality access tools, predominantly "dumb" terminals with no internal processing capability, prevailed and telecommu-

Don't look for a definition of client/ server; even the experts can't agree on one. Some see it as the death of the mainframe, some as a user-pretty system on every desk. All characterizations of client/server acknowledge three central principles: economics—exploit available technology to balance hardware, software, and communications costs by taking a Lego-block approach to building complex systems; organizational—use these building blocks to maximize flexibility and match systems to individual units' needs; technical—be aggressive in choice of low-cost, high-performance products and tools on a mix-and-match basis. There's no standard client/server solution because its very aim is to get away from the standard, narrow designs of the past.

nications links, largely existing telephone lines, were slow and expensive.

Reliance on mainframe computers has been greatly reduced with the development of exponentially more powerful and ever cheaper personal computers and workstations and high-speed local and wide-area telecommunications networks. The client/ server model exploits these resources.

- Clients are the decentralized, or "distributed," workstations used by those closest to the customer; they are equipped to do a considerable amount of processing locally, that is, independently of connections to other workstations or central mainframes.

- Servers are more powerful workstations that provide services and access to centralized stores of information and specialized resource-consuming capabilities.

- Telecommunications links connect clients with servers.

Consider, by way of a representative customer service business process, car loan processing. Computer and telecommunications systems are essential components of the process for evaluating the customer relationship and credit history, loan terms and conditions, payment arrangements, record keeping, and so forth. Prior to the client/server opportunity (it is more an opportunity in 1995 than a proven option; technical considerations render extraction of its full business potential a daunting task), the car loan application process involved paper and delays in equal, and usually substantial, amounts. The technology and economics of time rendered it impractical to process the entire transaction "on line," that is, while the customer waits. Today, of course, personal computers and workstations put enormous computing power at the fingertips of customer service agents, and telecommunications links afford immediate access to any and all needed information. Computer workstations are today hubs for information and transactions. At its most effective, client/server computing makes it seem that an organization's entire complement of systems, services, and information is accessible via a self-explanatory menu of options displayed on a workstation screen.

See also Front-Ending

Coach   The process movements almost universally see the role of manager shifting from supervisor and controller in a hierarchy to coordinator in a network. "Coach" has been deemed the term that best captures this new managerial ideal.

All of the process movements emphasize a newfound importance of the shop floor, customer contact point, and office worker, and a much greater need to draw on the skills and knowledge of these individuals. Indeed, effective process innovation is impossible otherwise, it being the people who do the work who best understand the process and how it might be improved for themselves, the company, and the customer. Study after study reports that managers are taken by surprise when they (often reluctantly) begin to listen to, and take seriously the inputs of, their staffs and are astonished by the energy, insight, and creativity their workers display.

What is a manager who is no longer the source of knowledge, driver of decisions, final authority, and "boss"? In the case of many middle managers, the answer is "an ex-employee." Process innovation rarely adds, and frequently displaces, managers at this level. Increased or more sophisticated technology and explicit decisions to downsize are the chief exit signs.

In the case of other managers, the answer is "a coach," a coordinator, motivator, and educator of a team of employees. The manager-to-coach transition alters fundamentally the labor-management relationship. Consider this instructive comment by a manager at Preston Trucking, an erstwhile poor performer characterized by high turnover and worker-management hostility that is today regarded as not only a business success but also a great place to work. Managers, he said, had to learn to "wear their egos around their ankles, instead of in their job titles." Preston worked aggressively to convert its managers into coaches and

We are at the end of the tradition of "manager knows best" and, hence, manager makes the decisions. The metaphor of the team coach captures the sense of what companies are moving toward: managers as goal and direction setters; players accorded full freedom and autonomy in how they apply their skills; and coach as a teacher and adviser, but still in charge.

Businesses, like people, collaborate when they believe that they will achieve a more desirable result working together than separately. Collaborators must respect and trust one another— keeping secrets and not meeting agreements, however informal, kills the spirit of collaboration—and bring competence and credibility to the table. Collaboration is the overarching issue in coordinating processes to realize improvements, whether through outsourcing (as collaboration rather than abdication of management responsibility), downsizing (as proactive positioning for effectiveness rather than naive cost-cutting), empowerment (as management guiding and workers deciding), learning (as sharing of skills and insights), or quality management (as multiskilled teams).

coordinators of empowered teams and individuals. The 25 percent that was unable to make the change seems consistent with broader experience across industries.

Collaborate   To collaborate is not the same as to cooperate, communicate, or participate; all are also forms of coordination, but only collaboration implies a purposive focus on goals. Nor is collaboration teamwork, although it may benefit from cooperation among independent individuals. Actors provide a helpful analogy. They in no way view themselves as part of a team yet must pool their talents and subordinate their egos in order to stage a play or make a film.

Collaboration rests on aggressive commitment to shared goals. It is generally most successful when those who engage in it are self-motivated and part of a professional or organizational community in which standards, practices, and qualifications are well defined and share a common language and set of assumptions. Academics, scientists, engineers, doctors, and investment bankers are examples. They may not like one another and be even less inclined to be part of a team, but they respect competence and relish results.

The distinction between collaboration and teamwork is important in process innovation. Collaborators are frequently a firm's source of innovation. Respecting their individualism is essential; they will not resist change, which, as innovators, they view as an objective, but are likely to shun teams, which they are inclined to regard as a straitjacket on their individuality.

Computer-Integrated Manufacturing (CIM)   Computer-integrated manufacturing (CIM) is the telecommunications- and computer-facilitated coordination of manufacturing from design to production. It extends computer-based process control to planning and scheduling and to the monitoring of progress and quality.

CIM is an immensely costly and complex technical venture. It involves first marrying hardware, software, and telecommunications facilities developed by different vendors on a host of technology bases spanning several generations of technical development and then ensuring that they constitute a productive union. The organizational challenges are even greater. Numbers of workers required to staff operations are sharply reduced, work styles and skills radically altered. The human element tends to be downplayed, and its importance diminished, whenever technology is permitted to drive the nature and pace of change. General Motors' deployment of robots in the context of CIM is widely acknowledged to have failed as a consequence of inattention to the human element. Success is far more likely when change is driven by education, team decision making, and conscious efforts to ensure absorption of the technology into work patterns.

Concurrent Engineering Concurrent engineering, the successor to sequential engineering, involves managing simultaneously rather than in a linear manner product or service design, development, production, marketing plans and programs, procurement, and other functions in the product/service life cycle. This both collapses time to market, an increasingly critical determinant of competitive success, and forces a cross-functional view of development. Concurrent engineering involves the development of a common framework for design representation and organizational continuity that is capable of integrating large amounts of diverse and complex information related to product form, function, and fabrication and to associated organizational and administrative procedures. It also requires significant investments in and commitment to productivity, reliability, and diagnostic-enhancing computer-based design and manufacturing systems and attendant networking and communications facilities as well as to new management techniques and organizational configurations.

Moving from sequential product development to concurrent engineering, as much a cultural as a managerial or a technical challenge, was the key to Boeing's and Chrysler's respective successful launches of the 767 and Neon. Years were trimmed from a process that costs approximately a billion dollars.

Continuous Improvement The total quality management movement holds that radical improvement derives from continuous incremental improvement, a notion widely known by its Japa-

Continuous improvement may seem a pallid strategy for innovation. But consider the long-term impacts of such improvement. Between 1870 and 1990, real growth in per capita income in the United States of 1.75 percent a year increased income from $2,200 to $18,300 per person. Had the growth rate been 1 percent less, U.S. per capita income would have been about the same in 1990 as that of Hungary, $5,500. It took Britain sixty years (from 1780) to double output per capita. The United States took thirty-four years (from 1880) to do so. South Korea took eleven years (from 1980). Sustained continuous improvement of 8 to 10 percent adds up to transformation over the course of a decade.

nese name, *kaizen,* which refers to continuous improvement at every level of the company and is characterized as an ascending staircase of small steps, each of which represents a short period of stability. The chairman of the aluminum giant, Alcoa, has neatly summarized the attitudinal differences that distinguish those who view change in terms of kaizen from those who pursue it from the business process reengineering perspective.

> Continuous improvement is exactly the right idea if you are the world leader in everything you do. It is a terrible thing if you are lagging in the world leadership benchmark. It is probably a disastrous idea if you are far behind the world standard. . . . We need rapid, quantum-leap movement. We cannot be satisfied to lay out a plan that will move us toward that existing world standard over some protracted period of time . . . because if we accept such a plan, we will never be the world leader. (Henry J. Johansson et al., *Business Process Re-engineering: Breakpoint Strategies for Market Dominance* [New York: John Wiley & Sons, 1993].)

Proponents of continuous improvement would argue that it is pursued within the context of a bold and enduring business vision and that radical change in any case requires many years of sustained effort. Among well-known examples of process excellence are Motorola's Six Sigma Quality program (which stipulates a defect rate of 1 in 3.4 million), Ford's Team Taurus project and "Quality is Job 1" program, and Xerox's quality management philosophy. These programs all involved quantum-leap shifts in management commitment and vision to generate momentum for organizational change, which was achieved over a period of years through sustained incremental improvements.

Coordination Costs   Theoretical work in economics—in characterizing as coordination costs functions that firms choose to manage internally and as transaction costs those they prefer to secure in the marketplace—has yielded one of the most useful and commonsense ways to think about business process improvement. Coordination can be defined as the management of inter-dependencies. Complex processes involve many elements of co-ordination, among them planning, management time (e.g., in budgeting), supervision, and interactions among those involved in accounting and performance monitoring. Each of these generates coordination costs.

Explicitly identifying coordination costs can highlight many real costs that are easily overlooked because neither the firm's accounting nor its reporting mechanisms attribute them to the process. Consider the case of one large firm that managed the building of new offices in-house because it had first-rate technical expertise and could match the prices of outside contractors. Or could it? It matched the transaction cost of using an outside contractor, that is, the price it would have to pay to have the project managed on a "turnkey" basis. But a significant amount of senior management and even board time was devoted to reviewing building projects, problems, and timetables. Add in "indirect" costs of administrative support and coordination among legal, finance, and other interested departments and it suddenly made sense to contract the work out.

Whether to manage a process in-house or buy it in the market depends heavily on coordination costs, which, because they tend to be viewed as "overhead" or "indirect" costs, are not construed to be an integral cost element. Viewed thus, process improvement is essentially an issue of choosing among different modes of coordination.

The distinction between coordination and transaction costs is a major topic in institutional economics, attended not only by abundant theory and mathematics but also by some important practical insights. One of these is that information technology, as it changes the options for managing interdependencies, also alters dramatically the nature of coordination costs. The substitution of information technology for humans in coordination largely explains the substantial cuts in middle management and supervisory ranks in recent years. Managing intercompany orders with

Organizations exist for the purpose of coordinating processes. How well they do so and which they direct management attention and resources to determine organizational effectiveness. The cost of coordination determines its efficiency. It is more important to be effective than efficient and even more important to be effective and efficient. It is no coincidence that so many of the most admired companies in business today, Wal-Mart being perhaps the supreme example, are both the premium service provider and the low-cost producer.

electronic data interchange and employing automated systems to track inventory levels and trigger orders takes people out of coordination loops. But information and telecommunications systems can also be used to bring them back in. Telecommunications-based systems create new modes of coordination; videoconferencing, groupware, and electronic mail, for example, enable teams to coordinate work from multiple locations. When it reduces the cost of obtaining information needed for decision making, information technology tends to promote centralization of processes. When it reduces coordination costs for customers and suppliers, it encourages decentralization.

The economics of coordination zeroes in on the most basic of business processes: coordination. How coordination is provided—whether through the use of teams or formal procedures, streamlining of workflows, deployment of information technology, or outsourcing—is an issue of process design. The costs of coordination are as much an issue of economics as the decision whether to incur those costs or pay transaction costs and go outside.

Coordination costs incurred by the buy versus make decision—of negotiation, purchasing and payment processes, and performance monitoring—have historically been substantial enough to encourage in-house production. But with purchasing, accounts payable, and accounting largely automated, much of the incentive to make is gone. Leading automakers today buy in a significant fraction of the value-added of their product, with enormous savings in coordination costs from the bloodless perspective of economics, and with painful losses of middle management, supervisory, and clerical jobs from the perspective of real people.

Core Competencies Core competencies, a term coined by professor/consultants Gary Hamel and C.K. Prahalad, whose work has had a significant impact on the theory and practice of business strategy, refer to a "bundle of skills and technologies" that enable a company to produce something of value for customers and to continue to do so over time and in the face of changes in the competitive marketplace. Sony produces many different products, some of which—the Walkman, for example—are major successes. Its core competencies support the design and production of superbly engineered consumer electronics devices that are small enough to fit into a pocket. Microsoft's core competencies support software development.

Core competencies are process based: Sony's design and engineering processes; Microsoft's recruitment, reward, and project management processes. They cannot be bought off the shelf. But consciously developed, nurtured, and sustained, they can become a major source of competitive differentiation. No rival has yet developed the core competencies that replicate McDonald's food service or Motorola's fast cycle time or Rubbermaid's product development. Theirs are what theorists in institutional economics term "dynamic capabilities" or "firm-specific assets." Such competencies represent investments over time that can yield sustainable competitive advantage in the form of a process edge.

Of course, changes in the environment can render today's core competencies tomorrow's liabilities. For decades, IBM's core competencies supported marketing to large companies and basic research. Today, IBM needs core competencies that support fast product development and consumer marketing, precisely what we find in Microsoft's repertoire of capabilities.

Proselytizers of the notion emphasize that business strategy should focus on building and exploiting core competencies rather than on forecasting or product and market or financial planning. From a process perspective, this means establishing—as an absolute priority—investment in the processes that embody the core competencies.

Core Process Core process, to the extent that it is used to describe business processes that are both common to an industry and a key element of operations, may be one of the most useless terms bandied-about in business today. It implies that processes

Core competencies, strategic intent, identity asset processes, the learning organization, sticking to your knitting, dynamic capabilities—all are different ways of stating the new obvious of business, that organizations thrive by building and sustaining a few highly focused mixtures of skills, technology, process design, and almost cultural obsession. They don't diffuse attention and effort.

To think in terms of the core processes of an industry is to be bound by self-limiting paradigms. All processes are not created equal; one insurance firm will handle claims processing as background, another will make it its identity process. A process predator will include another industry's basic processes in its own aggressive portfolio of innovations (which is how AT&T and Sears moved to leadership in credit cards, a "core" banking process). Customers don't care about industry boundaries; they won't decline British Airways' offer to make an international hotel reservation on the grounds that they have some moral duty to respect the hotel industry's core processes.

are largely industry specific and that firms in the same industry will share the same portfolio of processes.

Clearly, many processes are integral and inherent to an industry. A bank without ATM machines is not a bank. But do ATMs represent a core banking process? Viewed as "automated teller machines," they do. Solicit ideas for new uses for ATMs and the suggestions will invariably be cast in terms either of financial services or purchase of paper-based products: mutual funds and insurance or theater tickets and stamps.

Step back, though, and one can begin to see in the ATM a process infrastructure, a general-purpose access point for electronic services dispensed on the basis of customer identification by a card. Maryland's department of social service is using ATMs to electronically manage benefits (welfare and food stamps), New Jersey to process automobile registrations, and some colleges to handle class registration. Each of these applications uses banking's existing process infrastructures to render a new service at low cost. Business Process Investment terms this value builder "importing" a process; importing the ATM infrastructure in the service of its own processes did not make the State of Maryland a bank, but did transform its welfare payment processes.

Processes can be exported, too. A firm can use its own core process to offer, at low incremental cost, another industry's services. Thus, Fidelity Investments, a securities industry firm, and USAA, an insurance company, both exploit telephone-based service infrastructures and information technology capabilities to provide banking services with no physical branches.

Industry labels mean less and less in a process-driven world. Ford and General Motors are in the auto industry. Or are they? General Motors offers credit cards to customers and noncustomers alike; purchases accumulate credit toward the purchase of a GM car. Taken together, GM and Ford are the largest private holders of consumer credit in the United States. GM earns more from financing than from making automobiles in some years. Of the top three firms in credit cards, AT&T, Sears, and Citibank, only the latter is a true "bank."

Within industries, the same process can assume different levels of importance in constituent firms' business vision and strategic focus. Insurance companies' process infrastructure includes underwriting, claims processing, customer service, and marketing. All are core processes, but not all are key to all insurance providers. Consider four of the industry's leaders.

- UNUM, the industry leader in disability insurance, defines itself in terms of its processes for pricing risk. These are its identity asset processes. UNUM boasts that it can distinguish the relative risk of left-handed from right-handed New Jersey doctors who drive Volvos. Whether true or not, it makes the point that pricing is UNUM's key process. Branding is not. Whereas Prudential ("You own a piece of the rock") and State Farm ("State Farm is there") make branding central to their marketing, UNUM, because it sells through brokers, may not even be known to its customers.

- Progressive Insurance, a specialist in high-risk car insurance that accepts customers other providers avoid—drivers with histories of accidents and traffic offenses (it does not, of course, exclude drivers with unblemished records)—has used claims processing to become one of the most profitable firms in the industry. Its claims adjusters operate out of vans equipped with cellular communications links and computer workstations. Driving around their assigned territories, they may arrive at accident scenes before the police. Claims are often processed on the spot, sometimes even to the point of issuing a check before having the vehicle towed.

- State Farm's emphasis on branding relies on characterizing its network of agents as individuals.

Pricing is very much by the book, State Farm having sufficient customer volume to spread actuarial risk and price by category.

- USAA, perhaps the pinnacle of service in the industry, has made the customer contact process its principal asset. USAA prides itself on presenting a "single company image" and being easier to deal with than a next door agent. One telephone call gets a customer answers to just about every conceivable question and every available access to service. The company is the world's largest user of toll-free telephone numbers, by which it dispenses the bulk of its customer service.

All of these companies have the same overall mix of processes, but a different process is key to each. USAA's emphasis on its customer contact processes is appropriate to its core customer base: military and former military officers who represent a stable group of long-term reliable, trustworthy customers. Similarly, Progressive's emphasis on claims processing matches its predominant customer profile.

All of these companies are outstanding in the industry, each for a different reason. The notion of core processes tells one nothing about the differences, about how each company has created its own process advantage. Business processes are more usefully considered in terms of what Business Process Investment refers to as their salience, that is, their link to strategic intent and core competencies. BPI defines identity, priority, background, and mandated processes. Claims settlement is Progressive's identity process, USAA's priority process, and many insurers' background process.

Cost of Quality   Cost of quality is the *total* cost, including the cost of preventing or remedying defects, of ensuring that a product meets customer expectations.

Well-known quality management evangelist Philip Crosby argues, with Deming and Juran, that quality is free, that it incurs no added cost. Crosby's logic is that the cost of inspecting, reworking, and replacing goods and honoring warranty claims far exceeds the cost of getting a product right in the first place. He claims that defects cost most manufacturing firms 15 to 20 percent of their revenues. Others place the figure closer to 30 percent for service firms. By spending money to ensure, not repair, quality, a firm reduces its overall costs but also improves customer satisfaction and enhances its image.

Cost of quality thus has two components, the cost of conforming and the cost of not conforming to customer expectations and requirements. Included are costs associated with:

- prevention, that is, up-front activities, including design and training investment, intended to forestall failure;

- appraisal, including costs of inspection, auditing, and problem analysis and investments in continuous improvement;

- internal failure, including the cost of repairing or dumping defective products, making engineering design changes, handling customer complaints, issuing refunds, and honoring warranties;

- external failure, including the cost of making repairs to or substitutions for defective products in the field;

- exceeding customer requirements, including the cost of preparing brochures that customers throw away, buying advertising time that they ignore, and designing and incorporating features that they don't use; and

- lost opportunities, among them, dissatisfied customers.

These costs apply as much to services as to products. Moreover, they apply across the various process movements. Imagine, for example, teams organized to manage the cost of quality in

Warranty costs are a useful measure of the cost of poor quality and the impact of improving quality. In 1992, General Motors spent $2 billion, or $829 per vehicle, on warranty claims. One large dealer that had $2 million in claims for his Ford Lincoln-Mercury operations had such insignificant warranty claims for his Toyota dealerships that he began to offer Toyota customers free oil changes to persuade them to bring their cars in for maintenance. "So what the hell is this stuff about quality being Job One?" he asked (addressing Ford's advertising). The gaps between Japanese and U.S. quality redefined the basics of both economies. Closing that gap has redefined the basics of U.S. management. .

parallel with improving customer service and thereby achieving a powerful source of advantage: becoming the premium service or product provider *and* the low-cost producer.

Cross-Functional Teams   Processes cross functions. Companies are built around functions. Effective process innovation thus requires cost-functional teams. This is the new logic of organization.

Cross-functional really means cross-cultural. No one is surprised when differences in language, social norms, even gestures impede cooperation among multicultural team members. It is recognition that differences in departmental cultures can diminish internal effectiveness that has stimulated widespread interest in cross-functional teams. That such teams are often ineffective is testament to the intractability of the obstacles they are set to overcome. One is interfunctional disrespect; listen to engineers talk about "corporate" or sales reps talk about finance. Another is interfunctional ignorance; departments are seldom aware of one another's contributions to the firm, familiar with one another's technical language, or in command of an understanding of the process in its entirety. Business terminology and assumptions are highly functional or developed within the boundaries of specialized professional disciplines. Add to this source of separation that those brought together in cross-functional teams may see them as little more than exceptions to daily routine that add to their workload and their departments' costs and demand time-consuming orientation and training.

That said, process innovation relies on cross-functional teams for the simple reason that without them process knowledge is fragmented. Functional units' knowledge of the process chain seldom extends beyond the few components with which they interact directly. It takes a cross-functional team to effect the sharing of knowledge and insight implicit in the design of process change.

That the total quality management movement has served to provide a shared agenda and sense of purpose for such teams, to shape their missions and provide a common language that helps

"Mitsubishi organized itself for simultaneous decisions, instead of sequential ones, by using product-development teams that cut across departmental lines." In that deceptively simple sentence and its implicit contrast with U.S. car makers is contained the single major competitive battle of every industry: the vital need to break away from the often astonishingly tight historical, cultural, professional, and political constraints of functional fiefdoms. Since the process view is fundamentally cross-functional, cross-functional collaboration is essential for it to succeed.

to pull them together, may be because of, and not despite, TQM's own characteristic jargon and evangelism. Evangelism and excitement may serve as a mobilizing and focusing force for reengineering teams as well.

See also Total Quality Management (TQM)

Customer   The mantra of the process movements, "customer" and its attendant vocabulary reflect the underlying priority of process improvement: undertake process design from the customer's perspective and let customer criteria of quality, service, and satisfaction drive every element. Customer-driven quality, customer delight, customer needs, customer retention, customer understanding—too much emphasis on the terminology can mask tough questions that need to be asked at the outset of any effort to ensure customer-centered processes. Answers to questions such as the following are less self-evident than they might at first seem.

The customer drives. Nowhere is that more literally true than in the auto industry. That the previously successful Japanese missed out on the U.S. minivan and consumer truck markets was due mainly to their being too far away from the customer. Japanese executives' domestic customers drove necessarily small cars shorter distances on congested roads, had fewer possessions, and all in all were very different from U.S. customers.

- Who *is* the customer?

- What, *precisely*, are the customer's expectations?

- What does *satisfaction* mean to the customer?

- What, *specifically*, are the customer's needs.

Consider the first question: who *is* the customer? A customer is an entity that exchanges payment in some form for a desired product or service. But a customer is also part of a relationship, however short-lived and impersonal, with the provider, and the provider rarely has an exclusive franchise on the provision of a product or service. Effective process design must consider all three of these elements: the service/product offer, the customer/provider interaction, and the freedom of choice.

Who, then, is the customer of a consumer foods company? The immediate customer might be a supermarket or distributor, but the end customer with which the company wants a relationship is the shopper. Whose customer is the shopper—the consumer foods company's or the supermarket's? Leading retailers are exploiting overcapacity in supply to wrest control of the customer relationship from manufacturers. Branding and direct marketing represent process opportunities, even necessities, for producers that view the consumer as the customer. If, on the other hand, the retailer is perceived to be the customer, the manufacturer is probably well advised to direct process innovation at the supply chain and deemphasize branding.

Are students a university's customers? They are before they apply and are accepted for admission, while their options are still open. But once accepted, they are treated more as regulated users, whose participation in the university is subject to rules governing course selection and attendance, grading, and so forth. The "quality" of the education dispensed is largely determined by faculty whose imposition of academic standards, in the event that it results in a student failing, will likely yield a dissatisfied "customer."

The interests of a newspaper's customers can, and do, conflict. Is the readership more important than advertisers? Newspaper editors may, for example, face conflicts among serving the public's right to know (say, that a local company has been accused of pollution), considering the consequences of their actions (the mayor's fear that the paper's publishing the unsubstantiated accusation could alarm the community unnecessarily), and accommodating the bottom line (weighing the value of the company's advertising dollars to the newspaper's fiscal well-being).

The process improvement movements generally, and total quality management in particular, define the customer as more than just the buyer. Processes are characterized as having many internal customers. Each step in a sequence of process steps is the "customer" of the previous step, albeit often a captive customer. The notions of customer and customer power are somewhat vague in the internal context; it is the spirit rather the fact of being a customer that companies are promoting internally. Firms' information services functions, like their personnel and accounting support functions, are deemed to have customers, not "users," the term by which information services has historically known those it serves. Users are an abstraction to which information services need feel no obligation. To substitute "customer," "client," or "colleague" is supposed to make a service, a contractual obligation, or an organizational responsibility implicit. To keep the word "user" is to allow "quality" to be defined by information services, the supplier, in the same way that historically quality was defined in terms of product features.

Quality defined in terms of the customer relationship is premised on *customers'* expectations and wishes. In the "new" buyer-supplier relationship, the customer in effect tenders a request and the company responds with an offer, its set of services or products, whether fast food or consumer loans. The mix of service expectations that constitutes a customer's condition of satisfaction dictates that the relationship be based on matching offers and requests. This insight is the basis for a framework, one of the most useful for designing business processes, developed by Fernando Flores and colleagues, that characterizes every business process as a four-step loop: (1) a request by, or offer to, a customer (a manufacturer asks suppliers to bid on a contract; an ad announces an offer); (2) a negotiation that results in the supplier either rejecting the request or accepting it and committing to delivery (often an interactive process involving counteroffers and new requests); (3) delivery, which typically generates a series of requests, often internal, directed at fulfillment; (4) satisfying and, thereby, predisposing a repeat customer.

The third step is key if processes are viewed simply as workflows. It becomes secondary to the others when processes are deemed to be customer-driven. Then the question becomes not just how do we provide this service or how do we ensure a well-made product, but:

- What exactly is our business offer? What are we promising the customer?

- What is the customer request? With whom does it originate? To whom is it directed?

- What degree of flexibility is required to match request and offer? Who makes the counteroffer? Who accepts the request?

- What is the customer's condition of satisfaction? Is it realistic? Clearly understood?

Examined in these terms, the notion of "customer" assumes added depth. It provides a basis, for example, for analyzing the student-university relationship so as to be able to design processes in a way that treats students as true customers. There are widespread and well-documented concerns, for example, that in some universities, teaching students has become secondary to research and fund-raising. Untrained graduate assistants handle classes, the most senior professors do little classroom work, and the best teachers often are not granted tenure. The many universities that defend this practice are not viewing the student or his or her tuition-paying parent as the primary customer.

If it is accepted that the customer (whether internal or otherwise) is the reason for any process, then Flores' framework, as deceptively simple as it is powerful, becomes the starting point for process innovation: define the offer and request, create the negotiation space, and be clear about conditions of satisfaction.

In banking, a 5 percent increase in customer retention increases operating profits by 95 percent.

Customer Retention   There is a growing shift in the targeting of marketing process—from acquiring new to retaining existing customers. The marketing costs associated with attracting new customers can be enormous; the rewards that stand to be realized from preserving the existing customer base vaster still. It is estimated, for example, that a bank that increases customer retention by just 5 percent will increase its operating profits by 95 percent (the average retained customer provides 85% more profits than a new one). Similarly, a loyal customer of a car manufacturer represents lifetime sales of more than $300,000.

Yet marketing resources continue to be directed at attracting new customers. Hold up any magazine you subscribe to and count the subscription solicitations that fall out. By excluding them from its offer of a free Larry Bird video and substantial discount, *Sports Illustrated* is encouraging existing subscribers to let their subscriptions expire and subscribe anew, with attendant costs to the magazine for correspondence and mailing, billing, and account maintenance.

Customer retention processes are gaining favor with firms that recognize retention as the most effective investment. Such processes segment customers on the basis of demographics, uses of products or services, and profitability of the relationship in order to better target cross-selling efforts and special promotions and even to guide the design of new products to fill specific niches. Frequent flyer/buyer promotions are used to increase loyalty, and special services may be provided for loyal customers. Hotels, for instance, offer special check-in services for their frequent guests. American Airlines provides upgrades to first class with seventy-two-hour notice for Platinum AAdvantage members and twenty-four-hour notice for Gold members who are frequent, but not very frequent, fliers. Book clubs that offer four books for a dollar to entice new members also offer book dividends for existing members.

With customer satisfaction the priority of the process movements and customer focus the espoused basis for business process reengineering and total quality management, customer retention processes become a major target for process investment.

Deming, W. Edwards Still actively and aggressively promulgating, and emphatic in his advocacy of, the ideas that gave rise to the total quality management movement, W. Edwards Deming died in his nineties in 1993. The basis of the Deming method, as

Believing them to have become too isolated from the details of operations, Deming was generally cantankerous with senior business managers, to whom he would often say, "You don't even know what questions to ask." Seeing quality as basically a problem of top management, he was far more sympathetic to shop-floor workers. The Deming philosophy of management is to teach people how to work together, learn to trust one another, concentrate on the small results that over time add up to Very Big Wins, and use rigorous measurements to guide decision making and action. It's the last of these—discipline of measurement and management by fact—that distinguishes his thinking from that of many others.

it is widely known, is decision making based upon statistical principles. Deming defines fourteen principles.

1. Promote organizational constancy of purpose by preferring the long view to quarter-by-quarter reaction to the earnings report.

2. Learn the new philosophy of quality management.

3. Demand that statistical evidence of process control accompany critical parts from suppliers (Deming was among the first to highlight the interdependence of customer and supplier and the growing importance of the role of the purchasing manager).

4. Work closely with a small number of proven suppliers (principle #3 can be expected to drastically reduce the pool of suppliers).

5. Use statistical methods to determine the sources of problems.

6. Institute modern aids to on-the-job training.

7. Improve supervision.

8. Curb fear.

9. Dismantle barriers between departments.

10. Eliminate numerical goals, slogans, and such that divert attention and effort from the longer term goal of total quality everywhere.

11. Carefully review work standards.

12. Institute a massive training program for employees in simple but powerful statistical methods.

13. Institute a vigorous program for retraining people in new skills.

14. Create a structure in top management that will ensure day-to-day emphasis on the foregoing principles.

Discipline is implicit in the Deming method. Deming's decision making and implementation sequence for quality management, termed the Deming wheel, rotates through four recurring steps: plan, do, check, act.

See also Plan, Do, Check, Act; Total Quality Management

Deming Prize   The Deming Prize is Japan's most prestigious award for quality. Named after Dr. W. Edwards Deming, a founding father of the quality movement, the prize provided an organizing focus for companies' efforts to dramatically improve quality. The criteria for winning the prize, which amounted to a checklist of areas to address and of measures of performance, set new standards for Japanese firms, and the winners—recognized as being Japan's "best of the best"—provided later applicants with models to emulate and against which they could systematically compare themselves.

U.S. companies had long benchmarked only their relative performance against their main competition. The success of the Deming Prize in highlighting the best of the best and establishing new benchmarking standards, however, led to the creation of the Baldrige Award in the United States. The Baldrige specifically requires companies to benchmark their key activities in order to improve their understanding, encourage breakthrough approaches to process improvement, and set "stretch" objectives.

For decades, the Deming Prize was so highly regarded that even today, several Japanese manufacturers boast in their advertising that they had won it as long as thirty years before. Some may consider the award slightly less prestigious now that the high level of quality associated with manufacturing in Japan may no longer be considered a competitive edge but a competitive necessity. None, however, can deny the lessons it taught about investing in business process by setting the highest practical targets of achievement—by striving to become the best of the best.

See also Baldrige Award; Benchmarking; Deming, W. Edwards

Discontinuity   Change has generally been viewed as a curve, as shown in part 1 of the figure below. The slope, whether steep or

*The Fortune 500 list
originated in 1955. In
the next thirty years, 238
firms on the original list
disappeared. Five years
later, another 143 were
gone. In a period of
discontinuous change,
when the old rules no
longer hold, the most
dangerous management
act is to carry old
assumptions—and old
processes—into a new
environment.*

gentle, is continuous, driven by trends, rates of growth, and competition. Discontinuous change is a step shift in the nature of change, one that invalidates existing assumptions and revamps the rules of competition, as indicated in part 2 of the figure. Recent examples of discontinuous change include the complete breakdown of the communist bloc in Europe; such deregulation as NAFTA (the North American Free Trade Agreement); and the sudden convergence of the telephone, cable TV, publishing, and movie industries to create "multimedia" and the "Information Superhighway."

One effect of such discontinuities is to invalidate old assumptions, including those that underlie a firm's historical success, strategy, and culture. Processes that previously were valued as identity assets—the key differentiators of the firm to its customers and to its people and the basis for its success—now erode into liabilities. Examples are IBM's marketing and product-pricing processes and Sears' merchandising processes. Another effect is to force transformation, especially via acquisition: witness the race, in the wake of discontinuities created by the health care reform debate, among leading drug firms that specialized in R&D processes as their competitive differentiator to add new capabilities in generic drug selling, and witness the flurry of takeovers.

There are at least three types of response to discontinuity. The total quality management movement views discontinuity as simply a part of everyday change, requiring the same commitment, discipline, and sustained effort as that required by continuous change to carry the firm up the change curve. The business process reengineering movement sees discontinuity as a reason to abandon existing processes in favor of dramatically transforming the business through a step shift that gets ahead of the change curve. Process predators exploit discontinuity by breaking free of the confines of the process infrastructures that undergirded the established players' success during a period of continuous change (part 3 of the figure). A recent example is Direct Line, the British start-up company that, in a dramatic step-shift move, captured 10

Patterns of Change

1: Change as a Continuous Curve

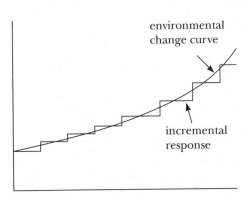

environmental
change curve

incremental
response

1a: Continuous environmental change

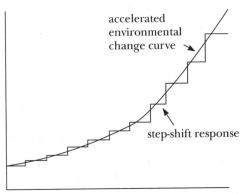

accelerated
environmental
change curve

step-shift response

1b: Continuous accelerated environmental change

2: Change as a Discontinuous Curve

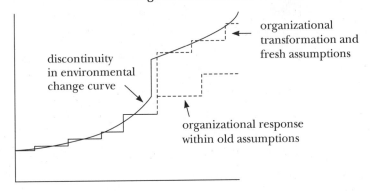

organizational
transformation and
fresh assumptions

discontinuity
in environmental
change curve

organizational response
within old assumptions

3: Discontinuous Change as Exploited by Process Predators

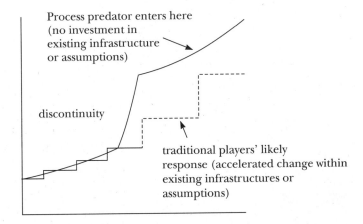

Process predator enters here
(no investment in
existing infrastructure
or assumptions)

discontinuity

traditional players' likely
response (accelerated change within
existing infrastructures or
assumptions)

percent of the auto insurance market in fewer than two years through telephone sales and service, involving no agents or brokers, as insurance companies struggled to diversify and make acquisitions in response to the discontinuity resulting from the nearly total deregulation of financial services.

In addition, as part 2 of the figure shows, a firm may be very tempted to consider a discontinuity merely a steeper change curve or to ignore how predators may exploit the discontinuity. An example might be a well-run European bank that handled the change curve of the 1970s through continuous improvement (figure 1a) and that of the 1980s, a period of accelerated change, through reengineering its customer service processes (figure 1b). But in the 1990s, a period of discontinuity created by information technology, overcapacity, global competition, deregulation, and volatility of interest and exchange rates, the bank continued its strategy by reengineering its branch processes. In fact, this is typical of the actions that British, Dutch, German, and French banks have taken, and in so doing they have lost out to predators that don't have branches.

In early 1995, Richard Branson, the flamboyant entrepreneur who founded the enormously successful Virgin Records and Virgin Atlantic airline, announced Virgin Direct, a firm that sells investment funds for personal pensions (the equivalent of IRAs). This operation uses the predator's typical tool, phones, as the base for service; turns upside down the industry's established pricing and fee structures; and changes the process of investment to drastically simplify internal operations. Only a few years before, Branson could not have launched his innovation, which rests on two discontinuities: the near-complete deregulation of Britain's financial services and the step-shift revamping of competition in telecommunications. In the face of these discontinuities, however, the existing competitors stuck to their old tools, unwittingly leaving Branson to fill the new vacuum.

Discontinuities change the rules of competition—both existing and new competition. Don't try to deal with them by applying the old rules faster or better. Rather, start challenging assumptions in order to drive strategic process change. The first question to ask is which elements of environmental change signal an impending discontinuity.

See also Business Process Reengineering; Total Quality Management (TQM)

Division of Labor Division of labor—specialization of tasks and roles, complex activities rendered as sets of simpler subunits, and a stable structure based on clearly defined functions and departments—is the foundation of the modern organization. The process improvement movements are nearly unanimous in challenging this traditional organization of work. Integration of labor, cross-functional processes, and self-managing teams are the (often temporary) hallmarks of organizational forms that would loose the shackles of hierarchy and the attendant division of labor mentality.

Division of labor is blamed on two prominent figures in the evolution of economics and business: Adam Smith and Frederick Taylor. Smith's classic statement on division of labor is quoted in many books and articles on process improvement.

> One man draws out the wire, another straights it, a third cuts it, a fourth points it, a fifth grinds it at the top for receiving the head: to make the head requires two or three distinct operations: to put it on is a peculiar business, to whiten the pins is another; it is even a trade by itself to put them into the paper; and the important business of making a pin is, in this manner, divided into about eighteen distinct operations, which, in some manufactories, are all performed by distinct hands, though in others the same man will sometimes perform two or three of them. (Adam Smith, *An Inquiry into the Nature and Causes of the Wealth of Nations* [New York: Modern Library, 1937].)

Easily one of the most influential figures in the history of economics, Smith developed the foundations of market econom-

Division of labor works well for stable tasks and predictable processes that can be broken down into discrete, self-contained steps. It's still the best way to run a restaurant, with management setting direction and supervisors coordinating operations. But it's poorly suited to contexts characterized by fluidity, unpredictability, and complexity. In such settings, it is better to organize by division of knowledge, bringing people together on projects or in cross-functional teams to work together in parallel instead of sequentially.

ics and laissez faire free trade and defined the concepts of social and individual "utility" (maximization of rational self-interest and well-being) that remain the foundations of traditional microeconomics and management science. His viewpoints are thus not just of historical relevance but timeless in their implications. Hence, it may be premature to dismiss division of labor as outmoded or pernicious.

Division of labor is as enduring a principle for increasing productivity as free market economics is for increasing social welfare. Smith demonstrated that division of labor generated far higher rates of output than would have been possible otherwise. He attributed the greater productivity to (1) specialization-induced improvements in dexterity, (2) time saved by not having to switch from one activity to another, and (3) the development of new machines and methods made practical by specialization. All three of these relate to repetition, the factor that links specialization to productivity.

Repetition and specialization were also the central themes of modern industrial engineering. Frederick Taylor, the immensely influential inventor of Scientific Management in the 1920s, is no less a target of the process improvement movements. Taylor has had bad press; he was by no means the fascist he is often portrayed to have been. He did establish principles, which became the basis of most manufacturing organizations, that exploited and reinforced division of labor. These distilled down to careful and comprehensive analysis of work and consequent specialization and standardization to remove causes of variation. Scientific management aimed to break work down into the narrowest possible repetitive tasks, eliminate worker discretion, and make efficiency management's primary target.

To Smith's enduring principles of organization and Taylor's principles of work processes was later added Max Weber's principles of hierarchy, which he termed "bureaucracy." About the same time that Taylor was becoming the most renowned consultant/

guru of his era and, perhaps, of modern times, Weber was pro-
posing that:

- organizations be built upon a clearly defined system of
  hierarchical relationships and employ a chain of
  command that equates discretionary authority with
  hierarchical level;

- organizations be governed by written rules and
  procedures that cover every level in the hierarchy; and

- jobs be assigned and workers promoted on the basis of
  technical competence.

The "modern" organization was built on the ethos of hierarchy and division of labor for very good reasons: proven results
that launched a true revolution in manufacturing, that enabled
the large corporations that thrived in the post–World War II era,
and that facilitated the mass production that brought low-cost
goods to a new class of people, "consumers." The principal limi-
tation of division of labor and specialization is that it relies on
standardized procedures and repetition; it is a framework for
managing in a stable environment. Its basic weakness, recognized
at its inception, is that it erects barriers to interfunctional coordination. "Bureaucracy's" positive Weberian connotation of the
professional, equitable organization has been lost and division of
labor has come to be regarded as the antithesis of innovation,
flexibility, collaboration, and adaptation.

With the search on for alternative forms of organization, it
has become fashionable to dismiss the traditional model as outmoded. Granted, it is less well-suited to a world of change, uncertainty, and the need for skilled, knowledgeable workers who, of
necessity, must assume greater responsibility for decision making.
There is no time to go through "channels"; standard procedures
can't cope with new situations; there is a pressing need to think
in terms of processes, which are intrinsically cross-functional.
Division of labor *is* antithetical to a process perspective.

But finding alternative forms will not be easy. There are forces at work in organizations that both preserve and generate division of labor. Complex work often demands specialization, it being impossible for one person to be an expert on everything or to combine the many skills required to be an effective generalist. Division of labor can even facilitate teamwork, a ready example being a football team, which relies on extreme specialization right down to the level of defensive linesmen who come in only in third-down passing situations; defense and offense are separate entities and train separately. Division of labor is the basis for the organization of a gourmet restaurant: pastry cook, sous-chef, maître-d', waiter, bus boy, and so forth. Finally, who today would argue with McDonald's way of organizing work, which is the epitome of processes built around division of labor.

Business process design is fundamentally about coordination of work. Division of labor impedes the coordination of work that demands flexibility or involves frequent cross-functional interactions and interdependencies. Such work can be made more effective through process redesign, a point made by many proponents of reengineering, teams, the learning organization, and total quality management. Division of labor may be the best mode of coordination in other contexts. Coordination is the issue, not division of labor.

It is worth reading Eliot Jaques, a highly respected writer on organizational design who argues that there are fundamental advantages to hierarchical organization and that the very nature of individuals' personalities, perceptions, and cognitive abilities make them most suited to and attracted to a particular level of organization. He believes that these naturally result in seven layers in an organization, each with different time horizons, and all built on division of labor. It is not implausible that we might, within a year or two, see best-selling books with titles such as *The Get-It-Done Corporation: Ending Team Paralysis* or *Competing in Space: The Third-Down Solution.*

Downsizing Downsizing is a response to perceived waste. Many U.S. companies have been overmanaged and overstaffed for decades. Nearly every survey of large organizations conducted between 1950 and 1980 showed middle management, corporate staff, and administrative functions growing far faster than jobs that directly generated business value. The watchword of business for most of this period was "growth"; "big is beautiful" and "bigger is better" became driving business principles. Conglomerate, synergy, acquisition, and expansion dominated management's vocabulary. IBM's chairman equated size and success when he announced that the firm would be a $100 billion enterprise before the 1990s. It got stuck, however, in the $60 billion range.

Business today, of course, is a different game. With growth no longer the key to increased revenues, profits, or productivity and size often the enemy, downsizing has become a necessity. Most often, it takes the form of a 20 percent cut in middle management, the bulge in the organizational pyramid. This simply reactive effort to cut costs usually achieves that end. But to improve effectiveness through downsizing, companies must cut out, or into, organizational layers more selectively or rely on creative exploitation of process innovation. Downsizing is often not the objective of the latter course, but a natural by-product. A reengineering project that reduces customer service time from three weeks to less than a day will eliminate people.

The more effective companies' applications of teams, worker empowerment, and learning, the more equivalent these become to cost-cutting through downsizing. This is not quite the message being communicated to workers about the benefits of teams, empowerment, and learning. Whereas managers are likely to see the process movements in terms of exciting and empowering management action, a book called *Every Employee's Guide to Business Processes* might interpret them very differently, in the manner of the following suggested definitions.

Downsizing is a springboard for survival for the oversized oligopolistic firm faced with new competition through deregulation, globalization, and efficient rivals. At issue is sales, profits, volumes, and so forth per employee. The successful firm leverages sales and profits per employee through a combination of downsizing, market growth, and process innovation. British Telecom illustrates the results. When it was privatized in 1984, the company had revenues of around $11 billion and profits of close to $2 billion. It cut employment in 1994 from 241,500 to 151,600, a drop of one third, and it more than doubled sales and tripled profits. Simple downsizing would have cut costs but not created innovation. Aggressive marketing, capital investment, and partnerships generated the latter.

Reengineering: a management justification for massive employee reductions and increased workloads for those who retain their jobs.

Customer service: lengthy stints answering the telephone and suffering eyestrain in front of a computer monitor after spending considerable uncompensated time learning to use the devices in conjunction with one another in the context of a radically different approach to dealing with customers.

Temps: what downsized companies call the people who used to work for them whom they now hire as needed at a fraction of their former salaries and with no benefits.

Empowerment: a euphemism for "You're fired."

Downsizing is inevitable, even essential in most firms, whether large or small, stagnant or growing, failing or thriving. The various process movements explain the whys and wherefores of outsourcing some processes and dramatically streamlining or reengineering others. The new directives are "stick to your knitting"; get out of businesses that are not key to your "strategic intent" or "core competencies"; and use information technology to exploit what we term the "Penzias axiom," which states that, over time, any person who gets between a customer and a computer system that can fully meet the customer's needs will be removed.

Historically, business managers have been educated to think in terms of and become experienced in upsizing: managing acquisitions, expansion, and growth. This is why most companies' downsizing programs seem amateur, ad hoc, and reactive, and why they get bad press. Downsizing as too often practiced leaves workers who are laid off feeling betrayed and those who are permitted to keep their jobs feeling demoralized. It's tough to be told after years of loyal service that your job shouldn't have been there in the first place, that "electronic data interchange" makes you and your experience and expertise irrelevant. It is also a copout for management to characterize downsizing in terms of the elimination of "jobs"; it is *people* who are being shed.

It is incumbent on those who embrace one or another of the principal process improvement movements to address the reality that downsizing will be a likely consequence of process change. It is not unreasonable to suggest that the downsizing process should itself be a target of process innovation or redesign, that firms should pursue total quality or team-based downsizing or reengineer the downsizing process.

It may well be that the era of wrenching downsizing—the slash-and-burn albeit badly, even urgently, needed elimination of employees—is drawing to a close as western business corrects its historical overstaffing, loss of focus, and organizational obesity. Recent works by a number of leading management thinkers focus on building instead of tearing down, Gary Hamel and C.K. Prahalad's book *Competing for the Future* being a notable example. Downsizing marks a firm as reacting to the past, as having not yet begun to hustle toward the future.

Dynamic Capabilities   Dynamic capabilities are long-term, firm-specific organizational assets that afford a company an operational edge that others cannot quickly acquire or imitate. Dynamic capabilities are embodied in processes; a special ability, flair, or skill becomes an asset only when it is turned into a process capability. Strategy, quality of people, and commitment to excellence mean little until they are embedded in a process in a way that renders it a source of sustainable business advantage.

"Dynamic capabilities" and related terms such as "organizational routines" and "firm-specific assets" are part of the language of research that spans economics and organization theory. They respond to the questions "What is a business process advantage?" and "Is it sustainable?"

The academic literature on dynamic capabilities and their variants demonstrates conclusively, if too often abstrusely, that the process movements are fundamentally sound and that business processes are, indeed, a central, even *the* central, determinant of business success. The literature considers companies that cultivated capabilities other companies cannot match and explores why these capabilities are so hard to imitate. The following are exemplary of its consistent and reliable findings.

- Differences in performance between leading and lagging firms in the same industry derive from the ability of the former to effectively combine people and technology in the coordination of basic organizational "routines." The case of McDonald's illustrates how difficult it can be for others to imitate the fruits of many years of investment and commitment. Surely it must be possible for other companies to duplicate McDonald's key processes. Yet none has done so. One company explicitly tried to replicate the McDonald's restaurant layout, procedures, and management structures, but it couldn't replicate the process capability.

- Linked to the foregoing is a difference in capital resource allocation. The leaders invest not just for the long-term but to build firm-specific capabilities. This renders the capital investment *process* a target of opportunity for reengineering, total quality management, and so forth.

The literature on dynamic capabilities is well grounded in theory and method. Too many applied and popular works on equivalent topics reach comparable conclusions by way of hype. Advocates of process improvement frequently pitch it to business audiences with warm and colorful jargon, not the coldly abstract terminology of institutional economics. To sell something "new" often means knocking everything extant as "old." Here is our parody of what is to be found in far too many business improvement books:

From (the Old)	To (the New, i.e., this book)
Fat, complacent organizations	Slender, aggressive organizations
Bureaucracy	Openness
Paranoia	Trust
Customer-hostility	Customer-empathy
The crisis of American business	The XYZ Corporation (see book title)
All you know about business is misguided	Read this book

The point of the parody is that the strengths of the process movements all too easily become their weaknesses; managers besieged by gimmicky titles, hype, overblown promises, and counterproductive simplifications are aware how much convictions can lose in translation. For every responsible vehicle conveying, say, total quality management there is the inevitable tailgater, hotrodder, or billboard popularizer.

The academic literature on dynamic capabilities is premised on scholarly enquiry and respect for history. It doesn't find the new only in the demise of the old, doesn't shrink-wrap tabloid messages, doesn't promise instant and global solutions, doesn't purvey fads that occasion backlashes. But because so much of it is intelligible only to members of university tenure review committees, it is the popularizers who get the business establishments' ear. As a consequence, reengineering and total quality management have been oversold and their promises too often unmet. The notion that teams are the answer to every business problem is beginning to lose favor. And the process paradox advanced in the Introduction is pervasive.

If one asks, "Mommy, is there really a business process advantage Santa Claus who'll bring me the organization of the future now?" the answer is, "No, Virginia, there isn't." Get on with your business process homework, though, because therein lie the dividends. Join a company committed to sustaining enduring dynamic process capabilities as an entree to the future or develop your own and follow that route yourself.

Economic Value-Added (EVA)   Economic value-added (EVA) is the after-tax cash flow generated by a business minus the cost of the capital it has deployed to generate that cash flow. Representing real profit versus paper profit, EVA underlies shareholder value, increasingly the main target of leading companies' strategies. Shareholders are the players who provide the firm with its capital; they invest to gain a return on that capital.

The concept of EVA is well established in financial theory, but only recently has the term moved into the mainstream of corporate finance, as more and more firms adopt it as the base for business planning and performance monitoring. There is growing evidence that EVA, not earnings, determines the value of a firm. The chairman of AT&T stated that the firm had found an almost perfect correlation over the past five years between its market value and EVA. Effective use of capital is the key to value; that message applies to business processes, too.

The main differences between EVA, earnings per share, return on assets, and discounted cash flow, the most common calculations, as a measure of performance are as follows:

- Earnings per share tells nothing about the cost of generating those profits. If the cost of capital (loans, bonds, equity) is, say, 15 percent, then a 14 percent earning is actually a reduction, not a gain, in economic value. Profits also increase taxes, thereby reducing cash flow, so that engineering profits through accounting tricks can drain economic value. As Bennett Stewart, the leading authority on EVA, comments, the real earnings are the equivalent of the money that owners of a well-run mom-and-pop business stash away in the cigar box. Renowned investor Warren Buffett calls these "owner's earnings": real cash flow after all taxes, interest, and other obligations have been paid.

- Return on assets is a more realistic measure of economic performance, but it ignores the cost of capital. In its most profitable year, for instance, IBM's return on assets was over 11 percent, but its cost of capital was almost 13 percent. Leading firms can obtain capital at low costs, via favorable interest rates and high stock prices, which they can then invest in their operations at decent rates of return on assets. That tempts them to expand without paying attention to the real return, economic value-added.

- Discounted cash flow is very close to economic value-added, with the discount rate being the cost of capital.

Determining a firm's cost of capital requires making two calculations, one simple and one complex. The simple one figures the cost of debt, which is the after-tax interest rate on loans and bonds. The more complex one estimates the cost of equity and involves analyzing shareholders' expected return implicit in the price they have paid to buy or hold their shares. Investors have the choice of buying risk-free Treasury bonds or investing in other, riskier securities. They obviously expect a higher return for higher risk. To attract investors, weak firms must offer a premium in the form of a lower stock price than stronger firms can command. This lower price amounts to the equivalent of a higher interest rate on loans and bonds; the investor's premium increases the firm's cost of capital.

The key business processes of the firm are capital. That fact is obscured by accounting systems that expense salaries, software development, rent, training, and other ongoing costs that are integral to a process capability and that treat the cost of displacing workers—a frequent by-product of process reengineering, downsizing, and the like—as an "extraordinary item" on the income statement. By treating processes as capital assets or liabilities,

Cash flow and the cost of capital employed to generate that flow have become the key determinants of business performance, with earnings per share increasingly a misleading or even damaging target for strategy and investment. When a firm switches from FIFO (first in, first out) to LIFO (last in, first out), its cost of goods assumes the price of the most recent purchases of materials in inventory. This typically reduces its profits because the older purchases cost less than the more recent ones. Yet the firm's stock price will rise, even though its reported profits drop, because it pays less in taxes, thus increasing its after-tax cash flow. The money spent to acquire the goods in inventory is exactly the same regardless of which method is used, but LIFO increases economic value-added.

firms can and should ensure that they directly contribute to economic value-added.

The following quotation summarizes the issues here. For "operations" in the first sentence, we can just as accurately substitute "business processes."

> How much capital is tied up in your operations? Even if you don't know the answer, you know what it consists of: what you paid for real estate, machines, vehicles and the like, plus working capital. But proponents of EVA say there's more. What about the money your company spends on R&D? On employee training? Those are investments meant to pay off for years, but accounting rules say you can't treat them that way; you have to call them expenses, like the amounts you spend on electricity. EVA proponents say forget the accounting rules. For internal purposes, call these things what they are: capital investments. No one can say what their useful life is, so make your best guess—say five years. It's truer than calling them expenses. ("The Real Key to Creating Wealth," *Fortune,* September 1993.)

See also Benefits of Process Improvements; Shareholder Value

EDI   *See* Electronic Data Interchange

Electronic Data Interchange (EDI)   Electronic data interchange (EDI) is the computer-to-computer transmission of messages without the sender and receiver needing to agree on a specific format. EDI has created immense opportunities to streamline processes. Consider, for example, the day-to-day processes involved in customer-supplier relationships, which hum along in a constant flow of paper (purchase orders, invoices, payments, shipment and insurance documentation, and the like) and multiple-step routines in many departments and tasks (data entry; mailroom; accounting; authorization; error checking; filing; computer processing of payments, receivables, inventory, reports). Processing a purchase order can often cost more than producing the item itself. Invoices alone can cost as much as $50 to process, according to many surveys.

EDI cuts out almost all the steps that stand between, say, the computer that prints out an order to a supplier and the supplier's computer that processes it and initiates production and delivery. None of these steps adds value. For example, 70 percent of all printed outputs from Levi-Strauss' computers are then input to another computer. Why not send the output directly from one computer to the other?

The answer typically went, "Because our purchase order and accounts receivable forms are totally different in format from our suppliers' order processing and invoice documents. There is no way we can get our 200 suppliers to change their formats to meet our requirements, and we certainly can't adapt our computer systems to handle all their formats."

Here's how EDI eliminates this problem. Say, for example, that a customer's document has the order number on line 1 and the terms of payment on line 21, while a supplier's document has the terms of payment on line 1 and the order number on line 6. An EDI message describes the document format so that it can be translated to and from the different specific data inputs required by the receiving computer. It will indicate that line 1 of the sender's message is "ORDER_NO", for instance. Of course, the parties must share definitions of terms and know, for example, that "DISC_30" means the figure that follows is a percentage discount for payment within thirty days. Individual industry groups have, in fact, standardized such definitions. The health insurance industry, for instance, after years of effort, established the ANSI X12 835 EDI standard that will save at least $10 billion annually in the cost of processing health insurance claims.

As with most process improvements that depend heavily on information technology, the main challenges are as much organizational as technical. The payoffs can be huge. By going electronic, McKesson reduced its purchasing department from over 300 people to 20, eliminating those who had been overseeing a paper flow. Many companies report cutting the cost of invoices from \$20–\$50 to less than \$1. The leading retailers are able to fine-tune their entire distribution system almost down to the hour, getting the right goods on the shelf in the right quantities at the right price.

It's not very convincing for managers to claim they are empowering workers when they are also eliminating jobs or maximizing their own four Ps—position, power, perks, and politics. The best firms appear to be those with a management ethos that trusts workers and secures their trust in return; that is demanding but honest; and that ensures that education, incentives, and measurements support empowered behavior. *Empowerment enabled from the top and diffused throughout all levels is what Toyota and FedEx have in common. In practice, in far too many companies, empowerment means either "you're fired" or "work harder with less staff and budget."*

Empowerment   Empowerment with respect to workers can be understood to mean either greater autonomy or greater responsibility. The two are quite different. Management that grants workers greater autonomy in the execution and mix of their tasks accepts that those who do the work know the most about it, that "manager knows best" is not the title of today's program. This response to today's fast-changing, process-driven world is rare; it leads to self-managing teams, "informated" workers, and managers who view themselves as "coaches" rather than supervisors or controllers.

More typically, management interprets empowerment as the delegation of greater responsibility for decision making to workers. When this is a consequence of downsizing or reengineering, the result is simply to spread the same workload among often far fewer individuals. Customer service agents, for example, might be "authorized" to see problems through to their resolution rather than go through "channels." This is as likely to make their work more stressful as more meaningful. Managers are given to characterizing the deployment of cross-functional teams and the inauguration of reengineering programs, actions clearly intended to reduce staff, as empowerment. It may be, but it translates to "you're fired."

Extended Enterprise   Many terms describe the links between firms and their suppliers and customers that are blurring the boundaries among them. Extended enterprises refers to companies that use information technology to create seamless flows of transactions, communication, and information. Electronic data interchange is the main tool for these exchanges.

Galeeb Toys, which uses IT as the base for its operations that rely on others' operations, exemplifies an extended enterprise at its most efficient. Galeeb links to its manufacturers electronically to place orders (thus avoiding paper up front); the manufacturers deliver directly to the customer (thus eliminating warehouses); and Galeeb makes and receives payments electronically (thereby avoiding paper at the end of the process too).

Many commentators see the organization of the 1990s as being based on selective outsourcing of activities peripheral to the firm's strategic identity and priorities, alliances with key suppliers and customers, and concentration of the firm's efforts on those few areas key to its success. Such an enterprise is extended both in its ability to operate speedily over large distances and across organizational boundaries and in its ability to combine its own strengths with those of its allies.

See also Electronic Data Interchange (EDI)

Fishbone Diagrams   *See* Cause-and-Effect Diagrams

Folklore Processes   Folklore processes persist beyond the reason for their creation, at which point they cease to generate value for a firm. They can and should be abandoned.

A classic instance of a folklore process is IBM's enduring dress code, which stipulated white shirts and solid-color suits. Implemented as a means of professionalizing sales staff at a time when the term "salesman" connoted peddlers, snake oil, and a fondness for liquor, the dress code complemented the company's rigid ban on the consumption of alcohol at company functions and during meals with customers. Sales reps for office equipment and computer manufacturers at the time were mainly technical people who preferred casual attire or old-style sellers who did not equate success with dressing like a banker. IBM's dress code was, in effect, a reengineering of the sales process.

As its relevance diminished, the code began to generate amusing stories, a sure signal that it was becoming folkloric. There was,

A manager in one of General Motors' suppliers that is linked to GM electronically for all orders and payments comments, "I'm not sure where GM ends and we begin. There's no boundary any more. Are we really part of GM?"

"Why do we do this?" "Because we've always done it." Or just "Because." Folklore processes such as IBM's dress code or the World Bank's styles of management presentation that demand lengthy reports instead of verbal delivery backed by viewgraphs reflect history—IBM's professionalization of the sales rep and the legendary Robert

McNamara's insistence on detailed information. Folklore processes can be as powerful and lasting as superstition about the number thirteen (most hotels still don't have a thirteenth floor). To lose folklore processes, companies must detach from their histories. Abandoning such processes is the cheapest form of process investment—if you can get staff to not feel compelled to add ten pages of statistics and to feel comfortable about leaving off their ties in the presence of the boss and pressing the elevator button for "13."

for example, the great Connecticut white shirt rush of the mid-1970s, occasioned by a senior IBM executive's visit to a customer whose offices were in the same building as one of IBM's technical support units. When an unshaven individual attired in jeans, sneakers, and a sports shirt joined them in the elevator, the executive asked his customer, "Why do you hire people like this?" The customer's reply—"He's one of yours"—prompted a next-day reminder that sent panicking staff hither and yon into the night searching for white shirts.

A 1993 book on IBM's troubles and the efforts of chairman Lou Gerstner and his management team to change its business culture and processes includes in its five-page index a reference to a senior executive's attempts to disenfranchise the dress code. Only when the top manager himself attended a trade show wearing a sweater and no jacket did employee's dress begin to change.

This example is a reminder of just how long-lived processes can be and how tenacious their hold. Folklore is part of culture and tradition, which are generally to be highly valued as sources of organizational stability and continuity. Folklore is stability ossified into rigidity.

Folklore processes are difficult to identify because they *are* folklore and seldom invite review. This is particularly true of reporting routines that generate computer printouts. Recipients who find them irrelevant presume that they are needed by someone else and the computer dutifully churns them out. A large consulting firm that discovered in a client's marketing organization a management information system report that seemed to have no relevance to 1994 operations determined that it had been designed in 1968 at the request of a manager who had died the same year.

In terms of relevance and need, folklore processes are dead. Bury them.

Franchise A distinctive business process, carefully developed and maintained and improved through attention to training and the review, refinement, and renewal of procedures, is a candidate for a franchise. H&R Block, McDonald's, and the fashion goods retailer Benetton are process franchises. Each provides qualified franchisees with a set of proven business processes.

One finds, for example, in McDonald's everywhere a remarkable consistency to the entire system, down to the food, mode of service, and details of operation. McDonald's protects these processes. It trains all franchisees and staff at McDonald's University. When it opened its Moscow restaurant, it moved in its processes; it sued its Paris franchisee for daring to change the recipe for Big Macs. It addresses every detail, the mark of the process-driven firm. In late October 1994, McDonald's authorized staff in its UK restaurants to vary the standardized farewell to customers. Because "Thank you. We look forward to seeing you again soon" sounded artificial in the context of Britain's regionalized modes of speech, local variations, such as "Eh, whacker. S'tha again soon," were permitted. The process is in the details; the process asset constitutes the franchise.

The key to Benetton's franchise is computer-based processes that enable the company to stock inventory and replenish shelves just in time. Benetton neither makes the goods it sends to franchised stores nor owns the stores. It is a process-driven firm that has turned its processes into a business.

During the recession of the 1980s, many previously successful middle and senior managers who were laid off or downsized or "counselled" out of their companies took their severance pay and looked for opportunities to establish their own businesses. To minimize investment, start-up costs, and risk, many bought franchises. That many of the very companies that had laid them off were at the same time looking to outsource as many functions as they could created a neat intersection of needs that spawned a new mini-industry of process franchises. There are franchises, many as old as McDonald's, that handle packaging and mailing, others that manage office cleaning, and still others that minister to office plants, all processes largely taken for granted.

We take for granted how many of America's most successful firms are franchised processes: McDonald's and H&R Block are obvious examples. Turning a process capability into a franchise isn't easy; the business must have a brand that stands for something for customer and franchisee alike and also must incorporate rigorous procedures, education, and support. The payoff, though, can be enormous.

Every company can usefully review its processes and ask:

- Do we have a unique slant on or bring a special capability to this process?
- Is there a market for it among other firms or consumers or, perhaps, as the basis of a business?
- Can we package and sell it?

A process for which the answers to all of these questions are in the affirmative might constitute the basis for a franchise that could be selectively offered to managers and staff being laid off. McDonald's, Benetton, and H&R Block have evolved extremely complex processes that demand large, complex companies to support their franchising. Tending office greenery is a simple process with enormous market potential.

Historically, computer systems were remote from the processes they enabled, executed, or supported. Hence, the term the "back office." Increasingly, process improvement rests on bringing the systems to the front office. An ATM puts the bank branch "in" the machine. Point-of-sale terminals put the retailer's inventory and replenishment processes "at" the checkout counter. In many instances—most instances for large firms—older systems

Front-Ending   In terms of the Business Process Investment framework, front-ending refers to making the existing corporate computer resource accessible to customer service staff through increasingly powerful workstations. But why stop at front-ending the technology? Maybe you can front-end the process. If the workstation makes information and transaction capability (e.g., order processing) accessible, why not pass the access along to the customer and bypass the customer service agent? FedEx provides free to many of its business customers Power Express PCs equipped with software that enables them to print shipping labels and track packages in transit. Everyone gains from this arrangement. FedEx is relieved of a significant volume of work and customers are afforded a new level of flexibility and service. When you bank with an ATM card, you are sparing your bank a teller or check transaction and enjoying the convenience of the service in return.

Viewing processes in terms of customers' rather than internal operational needs and priorities is one of the central themes of all the process movements. But most large firms' computer-based transaction processing systems were built around a model that relegates customers to the back end of an operational flow. Because it is rarely practical to discard these "legacy" systems whole-sale and rebuild them from scratch, they pose a major blockage to process redesign. Front-ending is one, and often the only, means to circumvent it.

But front-ending is neither a simple nor an inexpensive pro-position. The workstation component is readily available and relatively easily installed, but interfacing it to the installed base of computer systems, software, and telecommunications facilities can involve many complex technical details. The conceptual approach to its design and tools needed to implement front-ending are collectively termed "client/server" computing, a recent addition to the information technology vocabulary occasioned by the grow-ing need to provide interfaces at the customer, or "client," end built on the transaction processing software that interacts with the background, or "server," systems.

See also Client/Server Computing

Functional Organization Functional organization is the term used to describe the structure that manages complexity in busi-ness operations and environments. It is premised on three funda-mental and long-established principles: specialization and divi-sion of labor, hierarchy, and careful delineation of boundaries of authority and responsibility. How and how far to move from this well-established mode of organizing work is probably the single most complex and critical challenge for businesses today. Process innovation is fundamentally cross-functional in nature and spirit; the typical organization is not, in either.

The functional organization is designed to promote continu-ity and stability at all levels and to ensure that coordination is predictable. Activities and roles are defined as concisely as possi-ble, which facilitates decentralization. Business uncertainties and some inevitable overlapping of responsibilities are addressed pri-marily through some form of matrix management that balances functional organization with a secondary reporting relationship such as a regional or national organization. The aim of functional

can't easily be converted to do this. Microprocessor technology permits firms to leave these systems in place and use a computer workstation at the front end to eliminate barriers to service and process flexibility. Bell Atlantic is spending more than $2 billion to front end its complex, older customer provisioning systems and thereby transform these processes from back office "bureaucracy" to fast and responsive customer service.

organization is control; the mechanism for exerting it is the span of control.

The obvious problem of the functional organization is that control is a natural impediment to flexibility and flexibility, in a business environment characterized by increasingly rapid and wrenching change, has become a premium capability. Unable to adapt quickly, the functional organization tries to force fit new situations into old structures, often by ignoring or trying to dampen change. Similarly, elements of time, culture, local priorities, and physical location that mark the functional organization block, rather than facilitate, the intimate, flexible, adaptive coordination of interdependent units and people on which the effectiveness of key business processes increasingly depends.

Something must give, namely, hierarchy and the notion of jobs rigidly defined within functions. Some of the ideas and claims being floated in the management literature about the degree to which self-managing teams will supplant division of labor, empowered workers will undermine hierarchy, "coaches" will replace "bosses," and virtual will substitute for physical seem pretty far out. The books that exerted a sustained influence on management thought and practice from the 1930s to the 1980s were all fundamentally about the mechanisms by which organizations gain some degree of adaptive control over their chosen business environment, that is, about strategy, structure, decision making, management by objectives, socio-technical organization, forecasting, and such.

The notion of manager as decision maker has been central to this search for control. Early thinking emphasized the manager as administrator. The term "span of control" was coined in the 1920s. Business school thinking since World War II has focused on the executive as decision maker. The links between strategy and structure and the corresponding power of organizational structure as the basic management tool have been the convention for many decades. Peter Drucker, the intuitive genius whose views so often anticipate subsequent shifts in management style, early and explicitly posited management as the new elite that would be fundamental to the West's survival of the Communist threat. His position and most of the tradition that underlies the functional organization can be summarized as "management knows best."

Drucker recognized early the changes in every aspect of business, now so apparent, that are driving the shift from control to adaptation. He characterized the manager as the conductor of an orchestra, in charge, but a coordinator rather than a boss. This is very much in the spirit of the process improvement movements, philosophically if not always in practice. Managers do not know best. Change cannot be "managed." Cross-functional teams are of enduring, not transitional, importance. Hierarchy must not be permitted to block initiative and innovation. And all is paced, of course, not by company priorities and preferences, but by customer needs and prerogatives.

The functional organization is very capable of coordinating stable business processes in a stable environment; division of labor, derided by the wilder extremes of the process improvement movements, is highly efficient and effective. But stability is clearly not the order of business today, whether in markets, organizations, products, or customers. With instability becoming the rule, the task of coordination is altered fundamentally and with it requirements for organizing. Business books, from the 1920s to the 1980s, encouraged management to think about business in terms of entrenching stability and expanding control. Today's business books emphasize survival in the face of a presumed loss of control. "Chaos," once applied to isolated instances of undesirable instability, is today used to characterize the business environment generally, a circumstance reflected in book titles that present anarchy as solution, to wit, *The Age of Unreason, Thriving Amid Chaos, Liberation Management,* and *Managing on the Edge.* Learning is posited as the driver of organization.

That exaggeration bloats many of the attacks on functional organization and claims about the organizational forms that will supplant it in no way diminishes the insufficiency of process innovation to render a predominantly functionally structured firm truly customer focused. Not by flexibility and adaptability alone, but by these on top of the stability and continuity that functional organization assures, will the modern business enterprise prosper. Even the firms most bullish on the use of teams and widely acclaimed as being process driven remain fundamentally hierarchical, the difference being the emphasis of the hierarchy in management's role in facilitating and coordinating rather than passively controlling.

Only relatively small or newly established firms seem able to operate at the polar opposite of functional organization—adhocracy, the virtual corporation, self-empowered teams, and so forth—and these only for a few years. Apple, Tandem, Sun Microsystems, and other Silicon Valley entrepreneurial upstarts that a decade ago boasted a fresh, open, nonhierarchical, nonbureaucratic organizational style, with jeans the preferred dress even for the CEO, are today functionally organized. But there is a difference that suggests a need for attention to terminology as well as to organization. Perhaps discussion should be couched in terms not of organizational structure but of organizational coherence, with coherence understood to be the desired balance between stability and flexibility. Start-ups like Apple and Tandem rely on flexibility to thrive early and on some measure of stability to stay the course. Larger firms ossified by an excess of stability need a countervailing infusion of flexibility. The meaning of coherence is the same for both: the ability to accommodate change, which implies striving for effectiveness, and the capacity to conduct routine business, which is rooted in efficiency.

The difference between the stereotypical functional and more adaptive functional-plus-cross-functional organizations seems to be a project focus. In FedEx, Xerox, Ford, Motorola, and many other companies that have embraced team-based innovation and operation, a project is construed to be a mission-centered activity with a clear target goal and commitment to results. Projects may be short in duration (e.g., a task force), ongoing (e.g., a review group that meets periodically to address a specific goal-centered activity such as continuous quality improvement or customer satisfaction), longer term (e.g., a product development venture or reengineering program), or permanent.

The notion of a permanent project may seem a contradiction in terms, but there are examples of work that is always cross-functional, always mission centered, and always driven by an ethos of cooperation. The best of law firms, research and development organizations, information systems development groups, and consulting firms involve both functional areas and departments and specialist roles between which work, interpreted as knowledge rather than labor, is divided. Roles and hierarchy shift, with those who possess the requisite knowledge taking the lead at different stages. In a well-run information systems development project, for example, task leadership may alternate among the senior business analyst and the leader, senior technical designer, and individual members of the customer team. Seniority and title, though they still matter (witness the consequences for a "junior" who interrupts a "partner" in the course of a law team project meeting), are more pertinent to policy and decision making than to the details of working.

Business is ill served by polemics about the "evils" of hierarchy or of Adam Smith's invention of division of labor. To explore casting departments as permanent projects in project-driven organizations, cross-functional teams as one example of project coordination through division of knowledge, and of functions as projects in which coordination is better served by division of labor than by teams might yield more constructive insights.

In the functional tradition, the most effective way to get work done was by breaking it up. Today, more often the objective is to put it back together. To do so requires a culture of cooperation. But whatever form it takes, whether the contentious cooperation that often characterizes law and consulting firms, the relatively impersonal collaboration that marks many research and development projects, or that exceedingly rare commodity, genuine team spirit, what is wanted is an ethos of cooperation that spans levels of organization, specific roles and responsibilities, and attitudinal, experiential, linguistic, and locational differences. Traditional functional organization has tended to foster cooperation only *within* these.

Groupware Groupware, software designed to facilitate the location-independent coordination of work, has variously been employed to streamline processes, support teamwork, and enable parallel in place of sequential task execution. In a customer order process, for example, it might function as a sort of electronic supervisor, prodding engineering to deliver specifications and prices to finance and the latter, in turn, a customer contract to the sales rep. Groupware typically incorporates file access and coordination capabilities and provides electronic mail, bulletin board, conferencing, and reporting, among other, services.

Coordination is the core of business processes. Collaboration is the core of effective coordination. Groupware is an amalgam of computer and telecommunications software that handles the mechanics of coordination so as to facilitate collaboration.

Just as spreadsheet software revolutionized, in an evolutionary manner, analytic and planning processes that involve manipulation of matrices of numbers, groupware is influencing, gradually but fundamentally, the coordination of work that involves communication and information sharing among groups and teams. There will be no sudden, step-shift breakthrough, but over time groupware, Lotus Notes in particular, will change the very basics of coordination, and *that* is revolutionary. The coordination of complex work activities being the essence of processes, groupware is a source and catalyst of, and foundation for, opportunities for a process revolution.

Groupware marks a shift by leading software providers, notably Lotus, the creator of 1-2-3, and Microsoft, the dominant player in the industry, away from products designed for individual use on personal computers toward networked systems implemented as the basis of organizational communication, coordination, and teamwork. Such products are likely to stimulate in business processes the same degree of innovation the personal computer spurred in individual's work.

The many competing groupware concepts and tools are characteristic of the early stages of information technology–based innovation. In 1991, according to the respected Institute for the Future, a leader in groupware studies, 77 products offered some combination of what have come to be regarded as groupware capabilities: team scheduling; on-line screen sharing; group drafting; data and report sharing and conferencing; group management; message and data filing, retrieval, sorting, and filtering (the latter a key to avoiding the electronic equivalent of junk mail); meeting support; and workflow management. The number of products had grown to 140 by 1992 and almost doubled in 1993.

Articles touting groupware as the long-awaited revolution in organization that will put the knowledge worker on the information superhighway may be premature. It may be five or even ten years before groupware is as standardized and natural to use as word processing software, but it will, very likely after great effort and a great many mistakes and disappointments, become so.

The most likely candidate at the moment for primary enabler of global work, groupware represents as fundamental a shift in the use of information technology as precursor word processing and spreadsheet software. It also represents a major cultural shift that managers steeped in traditions of privacy, hierarchy, face-to-face meetings, and formal reporting may well find threatening. But recall that in the 1900s, the telephone was an entirely new means of communication, confined to a relatively small number of households and often restricted only to special use. Over time, of course, it entered virtually every home, and people came to use it for more and more activities, from casual conversations with friends to sophisticated telemarketing, to the extent that we now take it for granted. Just as today we can't easily envisage a world without phones, ten years from now businesses may find it hard to envisage a world without groupware.

Firms intent on breaking down hierarchies and creating empowered, team-based organizations that are not considering groupware are like firms in the 1980s that subscribed to the notion of superior customer service but ignored the medium of toll-free numbers. Team work is premised on interaction, which firms historically fostered through co-location. But moving people has become more costly in terms of time, expense, and quality of family life. The groupware principle keeps the people where they are and extends their faculties electronically.

See also Lotus Notes

Horizontal Corporation   Business processes have long been fitted to the structure of the vertical corporation, the traditional hierarchical pyramid. The process improvement movements turn this arrangement on its head, making structure a by-product of business processes. The new organizational forms suggested by these movements have in common: the elimination of chunks of the pyramid; the reduction of large units into smaller, more flexible, team-based, process-focused units; emphasis on cross-functional collaboration and communication; some degree of outsourcing; strengthened relationships with suppliers; dramatic upgrading of skills and education; and, above all, a focus on customers as the basis for process design.

A clear picture of the new, stable organizational forms that will evolve to replace the traditional, hierarchical, vertical organization is yet to emerge. Clearly, many managerial layers that have accumulated over the course of many decades are being scraped away by management acts of will, technology, and growing reliance on teams and empowerment. Management acts of will typically designate layers of middle management, administration, and organizational waste and eliminate them. Technology, particularly telecommunications, increases managers' effective span of control, a term too reminiscent of vertical organization that should be updated to "span of coordination." Teams introduce added flexibility and empowering individuals can eliminate the need for many minor functionaries and the layers they occupy in the hierarchy.

Business Week on a cover late in 1993 proclaimed: "Hierarchy is dying. In the new corporate model, you manage across—not up and down. Here's how." This introduction to the horizontal corporation vastly oversimplifies the most sustained, widespread, radical efforts to change the basics of organization since the 1930s. It also makes teams, decentralization, empowerment, lateral communication, and much else that isn't new sound new. The principal tenets of the horizontal corporation are to be found in the management literature of the 1920s. Vertical versus horizontal organization is a recurring theme because it involves an enduring tension between stability and flexibility.

Of the many imaginative proposals for new organizational forms, one or more perhaps will emerge as the equivalent of the multidivisional structure that was for so long the basis for balancing centralization with decentralization and stability with flexibility in organizations in which control was the overriding aim of management. Among the contenders are the starburst organization, a confederation of small, loosely coupled units clustered around a direction-setting central unit, and the shamrock organization, a centrally coordinated association of highly autonomous business units (one leaf), outsourced operations and relationships with key suppliers and other allies (the second leaf), and temporary workers and small subcontractors (the third leaf). The many firms moving in the direction of these organizational forms are looking for flexibility; how far they can go and maintain stability remains to be seen.

Business Week's summary of the seven key elements of the horizontal corporation captures the new management commonsense about organizing, but conveys little sense of what the end point will be ("The Horizontal Corporation," December 20, 1993). The horizontal corporation is a moving target, not yet a structure.

The Seven Key Elements of the Horizontal Corporation

1. Organize around a small number of key processes rather than around functions or departments; assure that each process has an owner who possesses authority and accountability for the process in its entirety.

2. Flatten the hierarchy by reducing supervision, eliminating waste and redundant work, and combining fragmented and streamlining processes in order to reduce steps and staffing requirements.

3. "Use teams to manage everything" seems far too extreme a statement, given that teams are not always the most effective or efficient mode of operation. Nevertheless, there is a trend in the direction of teams supplanting functional areas as the basic building blocks of organization.

4. Let customers drive performance and the metrics of rewards. This is the new truism of business.

5. Reward team, not just individual, performance. This is far more easily said than done and remains a challenge even in companies far along the path to team-based organization. How, for example, do you reward outstanding team *members* and how do you identify individual contributions while preserving the primacy of teamwork?

6. Maximize supplier and customer contact, by which is meant build relationships based on trust and communication rather than on contracts.

7. Inform and train all employees.

See also Cross-Functional Teams

House of Quality Quality Function Deployment (QFD) is a Japanese development within total quality management, the aim of which is to ensure that quality is designed into products and services from the start. The House of Quality, so called because schematically it resembles a house with a sloping roof (see figure), is a matrix designed as an aid to QFD. It is used to translate customer requirements into design and product features and communicate these in a simple and structured way that provides

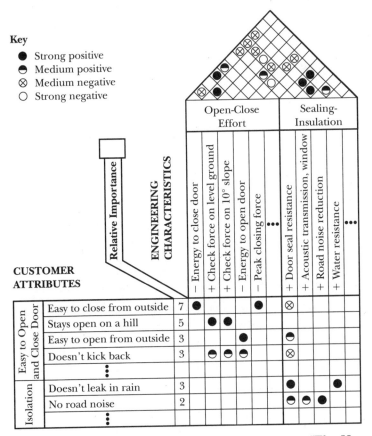

Key
● Strong positive
◓ Medium positive
⊗ Medium negative
○ Strong negative

Source: Adapted from John R. Hauser and Don Clausing, "The House of Quality," *Harvard Business School Review* (May–June 1988): 72.

teams with a shared language and map as the design process evolves. The matrix identifies customer expectations that cross-functional teams convert to specific product characteristics and functional area processes and includes an assessment of competing products.

QFD calls for marketing, design engineering, production, sales, procurement, and service support to work together on the initial design of a product or service. The House of Quality is a tool for pursuing this objective in a disciplined manner.

Discipline is a distinguishing feature of the total quality management movement that puts off many outsiders. To managers eager for "strategic" change and fast, flexible responses to the massive pressures exerted by the forces of change, too much of TQM looks like a metrics bureaucracy. The House of Quality is one such element. Hard to illustrate and likely to appear gimmicky at first glance, it is too often taken to be an end in itself, a complex matrix to be fleshed out with lists, numbers, and priorities.

It should be viewed instead as a reminder that process innovation is in the details. The House of Quality, like fishbone diagrams, control charts, and other elements of *kaizen,* the Japanese term for the ethos and practice of continuous improvement, emerged from many years of hands-on work improving quality. These tools share a focus on the nuts-and-bolts of processes at the most detailed levels of operations and what might be termed a "graphical team interface" (GTI), a deliberate analogy with graphical user interface (GUI), the key element in the deployment of personal computers. Within ten years of Apple Computer's introduction of its Macintosh product, every major personal computer and software application had adopted the Macintosh's GUI. The GUI, being simple and communicative, reduces the need for training and is responsive rather than restrictive.

The same ethos is essential for cross-functional work: a simple mode of team interaction, the ability to get under way without complex instructions, reliance on facilitators and translators (the traditional role of process consultants), and easy and reliable communication. The term graphical team interface is meant to capture what seems, in light of the established success of the TQM movement, to be a generalizable approach in tools such as the House of Quality to process innovation.

Hub The Business Process Investment framework employs "hub" as a verb to capture the single, most common element of successful redesign/reengineering of complex processes: to bring work flows to a single contact point at which they can be handled in their entirety rather than broken up and distributed among disparate functions and departments. It is made practical by information technology, specifically, powerful workstations linked via telecommunications to remote information sources and transaction processing services.

A well-known example that illustrates how hubbing can transform customer service is the financial services firm USAA, which has become the renowned leader in service through its provision of "one-stop shopping." A customer can call toll-free a service agent who can review on screen all of the information the firm has about the customer, including copies of handwritten letters (incoming correspondence is scanned and stored electronically). The agent can process a car loan application on the spot, in about five minutes for an established customer, and simultaneously issue a new insurance policy.

In business process reengineering parlance, service agents accorded such substantial discretion in handling customer requests are case managers. Case managers are responsible for multiple, related processes previously handled individually in separate functional areas. This represents not only significant organizational change, but fundamental change in the essence of work. It also involves complex technical planning, design, and implementation. Few companies possess a technical blueprint for the integrated infrastructures needed to hub information and transaction systems that would enable them to emulate the service levels achieved by USAA. The following diagram depicts two dimensions of an information technology platform's business functionality, (1) "reach," which defines who can directly access a firm's information and transaction services, and (2) "range," which stipulates which information can be *directly and automatically* shared across processes and functions.

Customers are included in USAA's reach. Many other firms match its reach, but none has comparable range, USAA providing for all information to be shared across all service processes. Most companies have developed multiple, incompatible data bases and software systems, which make hubbing, if not impossible, at least

Why should it take up to two months for a bank to process a mortgage application when only about eleven minutes of decision making are typically involved? The answer is that forms and the relevant processing move among departments and people, propagating the attendant overhead, delays, paper, duplication, and administration. If a customer service agent can sit at the end of the phone in front of a workstation and initiate the application, check the relevant credit and account records, and directly access relevant computer systems, then it is practical to make a conditional approval in about fifteen minutes. Hubbing, analogous to the practice in the airline industry, moves electronic "paper" to and from a central person, often called a case manager.

very difficult, necessitating investment in complex "front-end" systems.

The reach of a firm's information technology platform determines customer convenience, the ideal being for a customer to be able to contact a company at a personal moment of value regardless of location. Range translates to meeting the customer's condition of satisfaction, the ideal being a single contact that resolves promptly and completely any service request. Extended reach and range rely on hubbing.

Hubbing, being the natural evolution of information- and transaction-based services, is the logical evolutionary path for process innovation therein. Underlying every successful reengi-

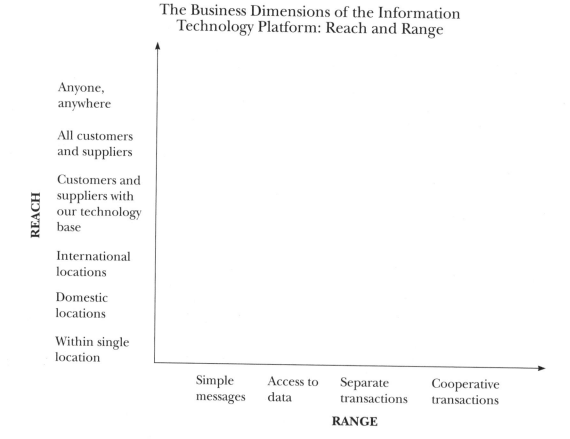

The Business Dimensions of the Information
Technology Platform: Reach and Range

neering effort is some form of hubbing for cross-functional processes. A firm's IT platform thus determines its basic business capabilities and renders process innovation and information technology planning interdependent.

See also Front-Ending; Integration

Identity Processes   Identity processes define a firm to its customers, investors, and itself. Not all firms have such processes and those that don't, lacking any distinctive, differentiating process capability tend to pursue "me too" strategies. FedEx's guaranteed on-time delivery processes, McDonald's fast-food processes, McKinsey's recruitment processes, Toyota's lean production processes, Motorola's "six sigma" quality processes, Nordstrom's customer service processes, and 3M's research and product innovation processes are all identity processes; in each instance, the processes stand for the company.

A part of the Business Process Investment framework, the concept of identity processes is closely allied to the notions of strategic intent, core competencies, and dynamic capabilities. Strategic intent is the overriding, single-minded commitment of a company's leaders to a specific direction or goal, the fulfillment of which relies on the firm's possession of the requisite core competencies or capabilities. McDonald's and Motorola's strategies are more than strategic direction; they involve personnel recruitment, training, motivation, and retention as well as coordination and management of key processes. These cannot be copied but must be built. Identity processes represent the fusion of strategic intent and core competencies that yield a firm-specific asset.

Identity processes are not always assets; they can depreciate, as they did for IBM, into liabilities. IBM lost its decades-long preeminence largely as a consequence of relying too long on eroding identity processes. The company's marketing and cultural processes—widely admired, envied by rivals, and worth a premium to customers—served it well throughout the 1970s. As late as 1986, *The IBM Way*, a book of tips about the company's

Which two to five processes do you, your customers, and your investors think of when your company is named? These define the identity of your business and its potential competitive differentiation. Companies that lack identity asset processes equivalent to those that support FedEx's guaranteed on-time delivery can only pursue a "me-too" strategy. Identity processes that have become liabilities, IBM's marketing and cultural processes are examples, signal an urgent need for transformation.

marketing processes written by a recently retired executive, was a best-selling business title. Think of IBM in the 1990s and its marketing and cultural processes still come to mind, but as the source of the company's identity problem, not an identity asset. Liabilities that drain value from the firm, they are today disdained by rivals. IBM's identity is imperiled and its leadership has yet to identify new identity processes, never mind turn them into firm-specific assets.

There are some obvious general principles for investing in identity processes.

- Protect identity assets through continuous improvement.

- Recognize that today's asset identity processes might become tomorrow's liability identity processes as change renders old assumptions and strategies obsolete.

- Move quickly and aggressively to rethink identity processes that have become liabilities.

See also Core Competencies; Dynamic Capabilities; Strategic Intent

Image Processing Image processing is the electronic scanning and storage of, and subsequent access to, paper documents. Because it attacks that organizational enemy, paper, image processing is, from a process perspective, one of the most important elements of information technology.

Paper flows are part of firms' historical reliance on well-defined functional areas and division of labor. An insurance application, for example, must be completed, find its way to the company's mailroom, and be routed to the department that enters it into a computer that generates another piece of paper for someone to examine (and return to the applicant in the event of an oversight).

Even in companies that rely heavily on computers, paper is everywhere. The next time you buy an airline ticket, watch how many ticket copies are paper clipped to some other piece of paper

Computers have barely tackled the challenge of managing information in organizations. The tiny fraction of the total information repository that is stored in computer files has been limited to data—numbers and alphabetic characters—and text—computer-generated word-processing files, electronic-mail messages, and such. Image processing has the potential to accommodate the remainder—forms, letters, diagrams, photos, and illustrations, the contents of filing cabinets, and the rest of the paper mountain. Image processing emptied three rooms of filing cabinets in one insurance company and has enabled Florida's land registration agency to locate and print in a few minutes documents that previously took several days to find and copy.

to be processed and stored separately. Exxon calculated in the mid-1980s that every original document in its head office was photocopied on average forty times and fifteen copies stored permanently. Management of paper often constrains service and efficiency and adds layers to administrative units; some estimate that paper management consumes as many as two layers of management in the typical large organization.

Image processing has the capacity to reduce waste, by eliminating the need to produce and store multiple copies of documents and to improve efficiency by making a single, scanned image universally accessible on demand. But it remains a relatively immature technology, employed by many companies for specific processes in individual functional areas, but by very few across all functions. One impediment to its penetration is the high cost, in time as well as money, of converting existing documents. John Gaulding, CEO of ADP's insurance claims processing organization, states with little exaggeration that when his firm decided to digitize its manual of auto parts it had to hire every firm in the United States that provided such services.

Image processing joins client/server computing and groupware as a core technology for process innovation. It does not create but rather enables many forms and degrees of innovation that are simply not possible when physical documents drive the process.

See also Client/Server Computing; Groupware

Import As used in the Business Process Investment framework, "import" refers to one of the most rewarding opportunities for companies to generate value through process innovation: to import a process from another industry. An example is the State of Maryland adopting bankings' ATM processes for its welfare benefit payment processes. The state used an established technology infrastructure with a proven and efficient process base to reduce errors, theft, and costs and simultaneously improve customer service. Used in supermarkets in much the same way as a credit

One of the most valuable contributions of the process view may turn out to be liberating managers from industry myopia. By benchmarking processes against the best of the best and viewing them from the customer's rather than the industry's (or public service sector's) perspective, managers can better spot such obvious opportunities as using ATMs to handle welfare benefit payments and college course registration.

card, its Independence ATM card has eliminated the need to physically process food stamps; store credit card scanners dial the U.S. Treasury's computer instead of a credit card provider's and check and update recipients' food stamp balance information.

This significant, yet in many ways simple, process innovation has become a pace-setter for other states. Maryland transformed its entire welfare benefits payments system by importing established banking processes and using the industry's technical base. Opportunities such as these are spotted only by organizations that are able to look beyond existing "core" processes, as the basis for analysis and comparison. Expanding the boundaries for benchmarking encourages fresh thinking about processes in generic terms.

Informate   Informate means to use information technology to enable workers to expand their understanding of their work and to be free to use that knowledge for decision making. It is a term coined by Shoshana Zuboff, a leading researcher on the effects of information technology on work and workers. Informate is the opposite of automate. Automation uses IT to remove workers' discretion and reduce their ability to influence a process.

Zuboff provides telling examples of the difference between informate and automate. Her main points are that the new systems often provide workers with a much broader view of a process than is available to their supervisors and that, if encouraged to use their new knowledge, workers can provide valuable insights and make effective decisions. If, however, managers view their own roles as ones of control in which they are the sole decision makers, then they automate the work instead of informating the worker. Zuboff doubts, however, that most managers will forgo their control and treat information technology as a knowledge resource for the people who do the work and know the most about it.

"Knowledge worker," a related term, crept into the management vocabulary in the 1980s, first to describe people who use computers in service industries and in offices. By now, with the process movement's new emphasis on knowledge at every level, the term has become almost equivalent to "worker."

Information Technology (IT) Information technology is a more encompassing descriptor than "computers" of the building blocks of the organizational information resource:

- information and service access tools, the principal ones today being telephones and personal computers (with interactive television a likely addition in the next three or so years);

- telecommunications links, including both local area networks (departmental communications links among personal computers, printers, and "servers" interconnected with other business units' internal networks) and wide area networks (national and international networks on the scale of the major networks, America On-Line, CompuServe, and the Internet being examples);

- processing engines, the systems that handle transactions and update records, that historically have been built on massive "mainframe" computers but that are increasingly "distributing" computer power across linked complexes of machines, each handling the part of the task it can do best; and

- information stores, electronic libraries of information, historically linked to "alphanumerics" (numbers and characters) but increasingly expanded to include "multimedia" (images of documents, video frames, photographs, essentially any information that can be captured and stored electronically).

See also Client/Server Computing

Information technology is no longer just "computers." Telecommunications has become the driving force for IT-based business opportunity. With telephone, personal computer, and, soon, television access to information and processing services, information is becoming truly "multi-" or, perhaps more descriptively, "omnimedia"; any information that can be coded in digital form can be processed, stored, and transmitted by any of these media.

Integration   Integration refers to making computers, telecommunications links, and information stores and access tools a unified resource. Information technology capabilities have historically been tailored to the needs of individual functional units and developed on a host of different technical bases that, until recently, have been highly "proprietary," that is, vendor- or system-specific. The emphasis today is on "open," or supplier-independent, systems. Because cross-functional processes require cross-functional information, process innovation without integration is heavily constrained.

Few companies possess an integrated information technology capability. The spirit of decentralized business decision making that most firms want to encourage also encourages decentralization, and thus incompatibility among the bits and pieces, of the information technology resource. Access to a bank's separate transaction processing systems and information bases for mortgages, consumer loans, checking and savings accounts, investments, and so forth might, for example, involve as many as twenty different telephone numbers. The same might hold for a manufacturing firm's separate processing systems and information bases for production, engineering, inventory, procurement, receivables and payables, and so forth.

This is the legacy of four decades of computer evolution. For much of this time, adding to incompatibility seemed inevitable. This is no longer the case. The term "seamless" is increasingly being used to describe the delivery of services to customers. Because manufacturing process integration, supply chain management, and cross-functional process reengineering rely on integrated work flows and, thus, on integrated information flows, technology integration must be a top management policy issue. It cannot be ignored, permitted to be impaired by individual business units' choices of technology, or delegated to the information services function.

Integration of the enterprise-wide information technology plat-

As a technical concept, integration is the extent to which different components of an organization's information technology base can work together. In this context, we speak of "compatibility," "interoperability," and "standards." From a business perspective, integration refers to making practical—in the face of disparate hardware, software, and telecommunications systems—the sharing of information across business processes. Incompatibility has for decades been the norm for IT. Integration is the goal, and very tough challenge, today.

form can be explained in terms of three dimensions of business capability: reach, range, and responsiveness.

1. Reach defines the accessibility of business processes in terms of a basic scale that runs from:

   - a specific company location during company office hours; to
   - our own locations to our other domestic locations; to
   - across all company locations, domestic and international; to
   - customers and suppliers with compatible technology; to
   - customers and suppliers regardless of their technology; to
   - anyone, anywhere, any time.

2. Range establishes which information can be shared directly and automatically across business processes on a scale from:

   - none; to
   - messages but not transaction capabilities; to
   - transaction capability within, but not across, data bases; to
   - transactions and information (but no shared electronic copies of documents, correspondence, or pictures); to
   - all information across all processes.

3. Responsiveness describes quality of service on a scale from:

   - batch processing (i.e., daily, weekly, or monthly processing); to
   - on-line (i.e., immediate) processing and access within set hours (notice that "we're open in New York

between 7 A.M. and 8 P.M." translates to 1 P.M. and 2 A.M. for Paris); to

- twenty-four-hour service (interrupted only by computer system "bugs," network "crashes," and maintenance requirements); to

- guaranteed perfection (i.e., no maintenance-occasioned downtime and instant recovery from bugs and crashes).

The business functionality of an IT platform is illustrated in the diagram below, which depicts integration from the company and customer perspectives. For customers, reach is interpreted in terms of convenience, range in terms of completion of a transaction with a single interaction, and responsiveness in terms of service quality and reliability. To go into detail about technical "standards," telecommunications "protocols," "open systems" philosophy, and other necessities for moving business from the chaos of multiple, disassociated technologies toward the integrated, high reach, range, and responsiveness enterprise-wide IT platform is beyond the scope of this glossary. The following questions suggest the principal issues with which business managers need to concern themselves.

- Given our commitment to business integration as a competitive imperative, do we have the technology platform needed to achieve it?

- Is our commitment to cross-functional, customer-centered reengineering of key processes and integration of our supply chain complemented by a corresponding commitment to cross-technology integration?

- Does our combination of reach, range, and responsiveness limit our degrees of business freedom—our range of practical business strategies and responses to current and potential competitors' initiatives?

- Do we understand our technological capabilities?

The Business Dimensions of the Information Technology
Platform: Reach, Range, and Responsiveness

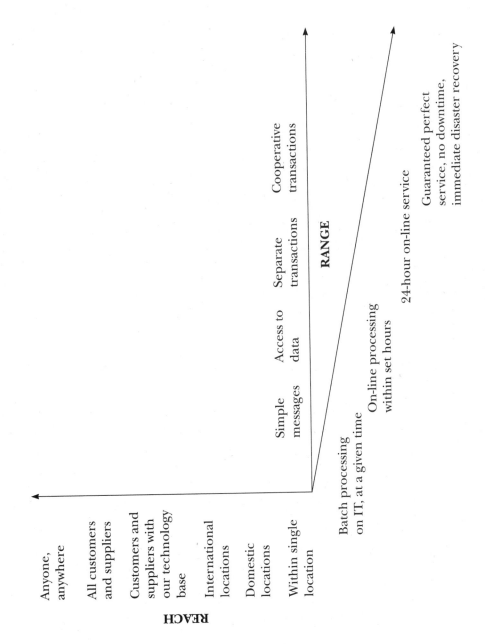

REACH

Anyone,
anywhere

All customers
and suppliers

Customers and
suppliers with
our technology
base

International
locations

Domestic
locations

Within single
location

Simple
messages

Access to
data

Separate
transactions

Cooperative
transactions

RANGE

Batch processing
on IT, at a given time

On-line processing
within set hours

24-hour on-line service

Guaranteed perfect
service, no downtime,
immediate disaster recovery

RESPONSIVENESS

If the answer to any of these questions is "I don't know," a more effective dialog may be needed between the business and technical sides of management. In this era of process improvement movements, just-in-time everything, cross-functional teams, and global coordination, information technology is essential to management. Managing technology has become secondary to managing the use of the technology, making it part of everyday business planning, development, and operations.

Business innovation in general and process innovation in particular relies on four key resources: people, capital, materials, and information technology. It is not coincidence that every firm respected for its process capabilities and customer service leadership is also highly regarded for its ability to mesh the management of business and technology.

ISO 9000 ISO 9000 is a set of rigorous quality requirements defined by the International Standards Organization. ISO certification is required of suppliers to many European governments and by the European Union (formerly the European Economic Community and more generally known as the Common Market).

The principal ISO standards, 9001, 9002, and 9003, call for documenting the conformance of quality systems to published quality systems requirements. They are, alas, heavily influenced by the EU's weighty bureaucracy. The link between customer and quality is presumed, not an explicit focus. There is no formal consideration of the relationship between conformance to quality standards and customer satisfaction, no reference to continuous improvement, and no discussion of business strategy.

The sequence of ISO 9000 registration is:

1. application to a registrar;

2. review by the registrar of quality systems documents and quality manual;

3. preassessment by the registrar and company to identify potential areas of noncompliance;

4. assessment, usually by two or three auditors over a two-
   to four-day period, that leads either to registration or
   to a period of "remediation" followed by a re-audit;

5. surveillance and period re-audits.

The U.S. Baldrige Award criteria for quality and the Japanese
tradition of kaizen stress competitive performance in a customer-
driven environment. ISO 9000 stresses conformity of specified
business operations to documented requirements. These are widely
diverging interpretations of "quality." ISO 9000 may be important
to a firm that does business in Europe, but it is not the basis for
a strategy that emphasizes total quality management.

See also Baldrige Award; Kaizen

Juran, Joseph M. Joseph M. Juran and rival W. Edwards Deming are most frequently associated with teaching Japanese business the principles of quality control that made them such fierce
competitors in manufacturing. Juran defined a Quality Trilogy as
follows.

- Quality planning: the process of preparing to meet
  quality goals. First, identify customers, both external and
  internal; then, define their needs and develop goods or
  services that meet those needs; and finally, establish
  quality goals that satisfy both suppliers and customers at
  minimum combined cost. The result of quality planning
  should be a process that can meet quality goals under
  operational conditions. (Juran carefully distinguishes
  operational from prototype or test-bed conditions; the
  test of quality control is the shop floor of a busy factory,
  not the laboratory.)

- Quality control: the process of meeting quality goals.
  Quality control involves choosing which variables to
  control, what to measure, and how to establish standards.
  Measuring performance against standards and ensuring
  that workers have the discretion and ability to resolve

differences between actual performance and the standard are the core of quality control.

- Quality improvement: the process of "breaking through to unprecedented levels of performance." This is accomplished by continuously identifying needed improvements, diagnosing problems, devising remedies, and implementing new controls that maintain gains under operational conditions. One of his principal insights, called Juran's Rule, is that problems will lie 85 percent of the time with the system and only 15 percent of the time with the worker.

Juran ascribes Japanese companies' success at making more and better products from the same materials and with the same equipment and facilities as their American competitors to the far greater number of quality improvement projects they complete. He claims that the average $5,000 to $20,000 quality improvement project generates $100,000 in cost reduction. The basic sequence is (1) identify and rank problems, (2) remedy the priority problems, and (3) lock in the gains. According to Kaoru Ishikawa, a Japanese expert on quality control, Japanese managers begin to worry that the improvement effort is stalling if *every* procedure associated with a particular process is not reworked and tightened within any six-month time period.

Juran sees his Quality Trilogy as three truly universal processes that stress unity and uniformity. It is easy to lose sight in the face of growing familiarity with the basic tenets of TQM, particularly considerations relative to top management's role in quality planning and the need for widespread and sustained education, of how very radical Juran's ideas were just ten or twenty years ago.

Just in Time (JIT)   Just-in-time production and inventory control was invented and perfected by a Toyota executive, Taiichi Ohno. It has become one of the core elements of Japanese quality control. Initially, JIT focused on eliminating waste. Ohno's brilliant process insight derived from a visit to a U.S. supermarket in the wake of World War II, a time when Japanese manufacturers' access to raw materials and foreign exchange was tightly constrained and shortages of inventory frequently restricted production. Ohno observed how the U.S. supermarket maintained a constant flow of goods, avoiding both excess and out of stock situations. He generalized this approach to manufacturing through the use of *kanban* (which translates to "signboard"), a communication tool built on a card that serves as part identifier and quantity indicator for incoming inventory. When inventory is depleted, the kanban card is returned to its point of origin where it becomes the order for replacement inventory.

Today, bar coding has replaced the card and inventory depletion and ordering are handled electronically, but the principle is unchanged: the elimination of waste in inventory. In retailing, JIT takes the form of quick response systems that reduce not only inventory and wasted space but also lost revenues and diminished profit margins resulting from the need to cut prices in order to move slow-selling goods as special sales items. Electronic payment systems reduce float, the gap between billing and payment or payment and expenditure. Float time wastes assets.

Ohno's main goal was to develop a system for making small numbers of many different car models, an essential strategy at the time given the small size of the Japanese market, lack of export capability, and dominance of the giant U.S. and European producers. In looking to cut waste, he took a process view that extended well beyond just-in-time inventory. Waste, Ohno recognized, plagued more than materials. He identified seven categories of waste (examples that apply to services as well as production are the authors' additions).

1. Overproduction, in the case of manufacturing, generates products that have to be discounted or stored in inventory; for services, this corresponds to excess capacity and overstaffing.

Just-in-time processes have been extended from parts delivery in manufacturing to service at the customer's moment of value, enabled by information and transaction processing capabilities that support immediate action. ATMs approve cash withdrawals just in time. Point-of-sale registers transmit goods-ordering information to the head office just in time. Moment of value specifies the instant at which a customer desires a service. When you apply for a car loan, the moment of value occurs while you are seated in the dealer's office. JIT information is essential to immediate (or nearly so) loan approval. The fifteen-minute mortgage is provided by more lending institutions every day.

2. Time spent at the machine and time spent inefficiently in a service process represent the same type of waste.

3. Shipping waste includes delays and redundant distribution steps.

4. Processing waste is occasioned by poorly designed workflows and rigid procedures.

5. Waste in inventory management is associated with administration and backlogs.

6. Departmental paper flows and paper chases constitute wasted motion.

7. Waste is also occasioned by poor service and the cost of repairing defective units.

Much of contemporary downsizing, outsourcing, and reengineering, regardless of company and industry, is a response to enormous waste built up over decades, variously manifested as overstaffing, excess management layers, complex and bureaucratic procedures, and lack of worker autonomy and discretion (the need to "go through channels" to get something obvious done).

First applied on a trial basis in 1952, JIT was rolled out throughout Toyota plants over a period of ten years and subsequently extended to suppliers and subcontractors.

Nothing is forever. Just-in-time systems are the new core of large-scale business operations and have greatly improved efficiency and reduced waste, but they create new problems. One relates to plant location. The long line of trucks waiting outside a plant must first get there, which is becoming increasingly difficult on clogged urban highways. When sales slump, as they have for the past few years in the Japanese car industry, too many models chasing too few customers can render the fine-tuned JIT system expensive. Moreover, the system is easily untuned; a strike in a plant or at a supplier firm that makes a single component can bring an entire manufacturing process to a halt, as can a rail or other freight system breakdown.

We are nevertheless entering an era of just-in-time everything, with customers increasingly expecting immediate processing of orders, next-day delivery of goods, and instantaneous completion of service transactions. Actor Carrie Fisher's wry comment stands as an epigram for our age: the trouble with instant gratification is that it is not fast enough.

From a process perspective, ensuring customer gratification as near instantly as is desired and practical is what drives JIT. To produce or deliver just in time requires careful attention to the details of a process, end-to-end. To make JIT the basis of Toyota's success took ten years. U.S. firms that have matched its success have required an equivalent amount of time to do so.

Kaizen   Many observers consider kaizen—a philosophy of ongoing improvement involving everyone, from top managers to the lowest level worker—to be the single most important element in Japan's competitive success in manufacturing. One commentator's characterization of kaizen distinguishes Japan's process-oriented view of thinking from the West's innovation- and results-oriented view. In practice, kaizen is a system for communicating ideas up and down the company hierarchy; everyone is encouraged to seek out and exploit new opportunities, and institutional barriers to the information flow are dismantled.

The kaizen attitude helps to explain why Japanese firms are so adept at exploiting new technology, even when they are not its originator. Kaizen-driven firms do not suffer from "not invented here" syndrome. Ideas are not the exclusive preserve of R&D, corporate planning, or market research; every new idea is welcomed and "channels" are forsaken.

An example of kaizen's effectiveness is Nissan's experience with welding robots. First introduced in 1973, within a decade their use had cut work time per unit by 60 percent and increased overall production efficiency by 20 percent. These gains were achieved through a series of kaizen programs that searched out improvements that cut time by as little as half a second. The

Characterizing kaizen as simply "continuous improvement" trivializes the concept and portrays it as cautious and lacking in imagination, a criticism frequently leveled by advocates of business process reengineering. More typically, the implementation of kaizen reflects a radical commitment to an entire way of operating that requires floor-to-ceiling change in management, work, manager-worker relationships, discipline, decision making, and the organization of knowledge that transforms an organization into a federation of problem solvers. Continuous improvement treats every variance from target as a problem to be solved and everyone as a responsible contributor.

programs, initiated within three to six months of one another, formed a staircase, each step occasioning a brief period of stability before the next rose, inexpensively, a little above it.

The logic of kaizen is that breakthroughs result not from massive reorganizations or large-scale investment projects but from the cumulative effects of successive incremental improvements. "Rebuilding a factory," wrote William H. Davidow and Michael S. Malone (*The Virtual Corporation* [New York: HarperBusiness, 1992], 118), "requires replacing almost every brick in the old plant. Do that too quickly and the structure will collapse. The only practical way is through kaizen."

That kaizen and business process reengineering are explicitly different philosophies is apparent in the contrast between the foregoing observation and Hammer and Champy's assessment of kaizen.

> To be sure, quality programs and reengineering share a number of common themes. They both recognize the importance of processes, and they both start from the needs of the process customer and work backwards from there. However, the two programs differ fundamentally. Quality programs work within the framework of a company's existing processes and seek to enhance them by means of what the Japanese call kaizen, or continuous incremental improvement. The aim is to do what we already do, only to do it better. Quality improvement seeks steady incremental improvement to process performance. Re-engineering, as we have seen, seeks breakthroughs, not by enhancing existing processes, but by discarding them and replacing them with entirely new ones. (Michael Hammer and James Champy, *Reengineering the Corporation: A Manifesto for Business Revolution* [New York: HarperBusiness, 1993], 49.)

The difference between kaizen and business process reengineering is fundamentally a difference in duration and magnitude of change; kaizen posits change as a sustained series of incremental adjustments, reengineering as an all-out commitment to wrenching reconstitution. Kaizen charges management to prioritize, standardize, and improve. Standardization and measurement are the keys to kaizen. Without detailed and specific metrics of quality and performance, there is no basis for moving forward; goals that cannot be measured are just rallying cries.

Kanban   Kanban is a Japanese system for managing production flows on a just-in-time basis. A major innovation in Japanese manufacturing, it is largely of historical interest today. The 3M company's version of kanban, dubbed "Nip and Tuck," neatly captures the system's aim. Kanban literally means "visible record." Initially a card attached to a parts lot, it is today more often a machine-readable tag such as a bar code. When the material accompanied by the kanban is depleted, it is returned, physically or electronically, to the supplying unit, which treats it as an order for replenishment.

See also Just in Time (JIT)

Lean Manufacturing   Lean manufacturing refers to a body of techniques employed by Japanese car makers to raise worker productivity and product quality to levels as much as three times higher than those achieved by their U.S. and European competitors. Toyota set the pace in lean production, Honda in lean product development. MIT professor Michael Cusumano elaborated the principles that guided these companies' innovative practices.

Lean production à la Toyota rests on eleven guiding principles.

1. Just-in-time production of small lots (in contrast to mass production à la Henry Ford, which relies on long production runs to minimize set-up costs).

2. Minimal in-process inventories (the core of just in time and a means to reduce working capital substantially).

3. Geographic concentration of assembly and parts, with delivery on very short notice by suppliers located close to the plant (this principle is breaking down as the manufacturers operate in more and more international locations and as growing truck traffic poses increasingly horrendous congestion and pollution problems).

Described by one commentator as "the exquisite refinement" of manufacturing, an adjectival phrase that captures its meticulous focus on details, continuous improvement, and use of statistical data to eliminate sources of waste, lean manufacturing is the basis of the Japanese miracle. Toyota, the inventor of lean production, is perhaps the single most outstanding firm in half a century in terms of sustained innovation and success. Exquisite may not be sufficient in coming decades, even for Toyota. Nimbleness will be required as well. Agile manufacturing is the next evolution of manufacturing.

4. The use of kanban cards to track and control inventory needs at each stage of production (a key to just-in-time inventory management; Toyota's original manual kanban system is still widely used in Japan even as bar code scanners are increasingly replacing cards).

5. Production leveling (building flexibility and speed into operations in order to maintain full capacity production with minimal wastage and downtime).

6. Rapid setup (the key to reducing the length of production runs without driving up costs).

7. Work standardization (standards and supporting statistical quality control data, and a superbly trained labor force, are fundamental to total quality management).

8. Multiskilled workers (the competitive differentiator in nearly every economy today).

9. Selective use of automation (Japanese companies in general avoided large-scale data processing and robotics projects such as the $54 billion debacle by General Motors, whose chairman could have bought the entire Japanese car industry for just $35 billion. Taiichi Ohno, the genius behind Toyota's lean production, recognizing the potential of technology to introduce rigidity on the production line, set adaptability and support of such production elements as short runs and rapid setup as criteria for applications of it).

10. Heavy reliance on subcontracting (the flexibility this afforded in operations enabled Toyota to pressure suppliers to cut their costs—which constitute around 75 percent of the total manufacturing cost—and improve quality).

11. Continuous incremental improvement (the ethos of total quality management, disdained by radical change-seeking business process reengineering).

Cusumano identified an equal number of principles underlying lean product development à la Honda.

1. Rapid model changes (42 months in development compared to 64 months for top American and European firms).

2. Frequent expansion of product ranges (the nine major Japanese car makers replaced models every four years, main foreign competitors every six to eight years).

3. Overlapping and compressed development phases (extended by American manufacturers to include concurrent engineering, development of the Ford Taurus being exemplary).

4. High levels of supplier engineering, small numbers of suppliers engaged in long-term relationships and collaborative alliances (plus large numbers of component suppliers extorted on price and delivery conditions).

5. "Heavyweight" project managers (with the clout to ensure that cross-functional teams are backed by authority and leadership).

6. Continuity of design teams and managers to preserve accountability and relationships throughout the life of a project (contrast this with problematic long-term U.S. military projects in which the colonel assigned responsibility ignores cost overruns until he or she finds someone to take over the white elephant).

7. Strict engineering schedules and work disciplines.

8. Superior communication mechanisms and skills (middle management, viewed in U.S. firms not as the

key bridge between workers and senior executives that is the Japanese perspective, but as an impediment to communication and change and an American endangered species).

9. Multiskilled engineers and design teams.

10. Computer-aided design tools.

11. Continuous incremental improvement (consistent with Japan's conception of total quality management).

That these process-based disciplines are no longer the distinctive domain of Japanese manufacturers is evidenced by American car makers' appropriation of Honda's concurrent engineering practices and Toyota's total quality management philosophy. The Japanese edge is being further eroded by emerging constraints of lean manufacturing. Lean production is running up against urban congestion, debilitating stress on suppliers, excessive product variety and a shortage of blue-collar workers (Toyota's annual turnover is 30 percent), lean product development against the high cost of model replacement (exacerbated by a shrinking market), environmental and recycling costs, and, like lean production, excessive product variety. Fewer younger workers, moreover, are willing to work the hours demanded or accept the discipline imposed by lean manufacturing.

See also Continuous Improvement; Concurrent Engineering; Cross-Functional Teams; Just in Time; Kanban

Learning Organization   Peter Senge in *The Fifth Discipline* uses the term learning organization to capture a widely recognized priority for process innovation: to effect a degree of organizational flexibility and responsiveness that fosters novel perspectives cooperatively introduced into every element of operations. The learning organization empowers its workers, opens its channels of communication, and exhibits a willingness to abandon old assumptions and habits. It exhibits five "component technologies."

Learning is the new currency of work in an era of continuing change and uncertainty and fewer workers burdened with more complex responsibilities in downsized, technology-driven, collaborative organizations. There's a big difference between learning and being taught. Those who listen to teachers and prepare for and complete exams and papers have really only learned to be taught. They also disproportionately populate company training programs. The learning organization will need talented learners—people who have learned how to

1. Systems thinking: emphasis on dynamic interrelationships among business factors over highly compartmentalized departmental views of the most immediate and visible elements of the environment.

2. Personal mastery: investments in individual and organizational learning to prevent experience from atrophying and curiosity from being stifled as job requirements are met instead of exceeded.

3. Mental models: lateral and nonlinear thinking.

4. Shared vision.

5. Team learning.

Senge argues for metanoia: a shift in mind. He contends that organizations learn poorly, that their "cultures" are seldom more than mental sets of shared, unchallenged assumptions, perceptions, and rote actions. Learning is blocked, he suggests, by the notions that "I am my position" and "the enemy is out there," by the illusion of being in charge of change, by fixation on events (rather than on continuing processes that underlie events), and by the myth of the top management "team." Senge finds the sources of today's problems in yesterday's solutions. People in learning organizations see beyond simple cause-and-effect linear chains to interrelationships and dynamic complexity. Learning is a team skill that requires vision and experimentation.

Senge doesn't include in the index to his book the terms "process" or "reengineering," but many of the principles he relates are viewed by proponents of business process reengineering and total quality management as essential organizational underpinnings—namely, the learning organization and the learning individual—of the tools and techniques they recommend. It is a truism that change is changing; one does not so much "manage" it as abandon old, often previously successful assumptions and processes to accommodate it, a more difficult task by far. If workers and managers must be able to collaboratively generate new

learn, who are inquisitive and adaptable, willing to tackle tough subjects, and personally committed to growth. One of the world's best-performing banks concluded that only 10 percent of its staff possessed the talent, flexibility, and tolerance for ambiguity to be real learners; 70 percent would learn only if taught; and 20 percent were stuck and could not change.

Johnson and Higgins arranges insurance coverage for many of the world's largest firms. Lotus Notes enables its 2,700 brokers in eighty-five countries to exchange ideas as if they were in the same room. "It's the biggest brainstorming session going," remarked one manager. "You often find a problem you face has already been solved by somebody else." Brokers access shared, topical databases and news feeds; secretaries log correspondence by category and project; managers track progress, problems, and queries. Notes manages the details.

insights that turn shared visions into reality, it may be that the learning process itself is the most important one to reengineer.

Lotus Notes Lotus Notes is perhaps the leading example of a "groupware" or "workflow" product widely used to stimulate, enable, or support substantive process innovation. It facilitates the coordination of process steps, interpersonal interactions, and information sharing. Processes being fundamentally about coordination, such tools are becoming a cornerstone of improvement efforts. Frequent applications include the linking of sales to production, streamlining of customer service and administration, and management of project teams distributed geographically, temporally, or both.

By far the leading product in the groupware market, Lotus Notes is viewed by a growing number of firms as a basis for rethinking many aspects of basic organization. Notes includes practically every computer-based facility a group or team might need, but its installation is daunting and use complex, an almost inevitable consequence of its power and scope. It supports as near to a networked office as exists today, enabling staff in different buildings, states, and even countries to work together as if they were in the same room.

See also Groupware

BancOne's more than 400 branches are ranked monthly by facts about service and economic performance: number of new CD accounts opened, average time to process a loan

Management by Fact A fundamental tenet of the founders and most successful practitioners of total quality management is management by fact instead of by opinion. Such management relies on metrics as the bases for assessing performance and progress and for guiding problem solving and process improvement. All the companies best known for quality have created a discipline built around metrics, not as a bureaucracy but as a vehicle for rigor and objectivity. A small set of metrics, defined and shared by management and workers alike as the key indicators to guide improvement (and often to determine rewards), becomes almost a cultural driver; think of FedEx's guaranteed on-time delivery, which is not just a vague goal but a precisely monitored quality metric.

Of course, it is far easier to identify the "facts" to manage by in manufacturing than in service industries. What exactly is customer "satisfaction" or "service," for instance? Many service organizations simply do not have facts to manage by: they lack the operational data needed for process improvement. The adage that if you can't measure it, you can't improve it seems a valid one for quality management.

See also Total Quality Management (TQM); Toyota's "Five Whys"

Mandated Processes Mandated processes are just that: business processes that are required as, for example, to satisfy regulatory reporting requirements or ensure compliance with tax law. They seldom add value and can consume enormous resources (the *basic* federal income tax forms filed by a Fortune 1000 company if laid one on top of another would reach a height of more than eight feet).

In the Business Process Investment scheme of things, mandated processes are liability processes. Reengineering can make such processes less expensive, but it cannot make them add value and it *will* divert resources, time, and management attention from investment opportunities that offer greater potential payoff. BPI thus directs firms to outsource mandated processes.

Tax compliance processes are not mandated liability processes for every firm. For Bix Six accounting firms, they are priority asset processes. When firms improve these processes, they improve business performance. It thus made eminent sense for British Petroleum to outsource its tax compliance processes to Arthur Andersen and Coopers & Lybrand. It could do so with assurance that the latter has every incentive to maintain the very best tax compliance processes.

The literature on total quality management, the learning organization, and business process reengineering does not address mandated processes. They fall outside their primary focus, which

application, staff productivity. These metrics are published across the firm, allowing a manager who is ranked low on a particular metric to identify and contact a comparable but high-performing branch. The purpose of the metrics is not to control or punish but to provide a base for management by fact.

That regulation and government reporting and corresponding paperwork is a growing burden on almost all companies is no secret to managers. These mandated processes, being economic liabilities, are candidates for outsourcing to firms for which they are the core business thrust and strength. Thus, British Petroleum outsourced its tax compliance processes to Big Six accounting firms.

is on processes that are relevant to customer service. It's well worthwhile for managers to look at their firm's operations in order to outsource mandated processes. These cannot, by definition, be gotten rid of, nor can they be made to yield value. Let a firm that has made them asset processes handle them and make money doing so.

See also Identity Processes

Mass Customization   Mass customization is the tailoring of a large-scale production product or service—an automobile, financial service, or publication, for example—to individual customers. It marries low cost achieved through lean, standardized, volume production of components with the flexibility, responsiveness, and service demanded by customers who have a plethora of choices in products and services and their suppliers.

Mass customization is not an oxymoron, the business equivalent of jumbo shrimp. Overcapacity and commoditization, among other forces, have rendered satisfaction of individual customer wants and needs, and, hence, customization, the principal source of competitive differentiation, while simultaneously exerting tremendous pressure on prices, costs, and margins, which can be accommodated only by minimizing variety as much as possible. Mass customization seeks to strike a balance between these two ends.

To understand the information requirements that attend mass customization, imagine what a telephone/mail-order retailer such as Lands' End needs to know in order to customize its catalogs to individual consumers' purchase patterns, or what is required for Nissan to deliver the three-day automobile (whereby customer specifications selected at a showroom computer are entered directly into Nissan's production schedule and the customized vehicle rolled off the mass production line and delivered, all within three days). A handful of financial services firms have integrated (and most others are striving to integrate) information on service requirements, demographic details, and profitability of individual customer relationships into customer profiles that can be used to

Customer power and choice demand customization. The economics of doing business in a just-in-time environment characterized by eroding margins, overcapacity, and commoditization push firms toward standardization. Mass customization is the new art form. The best personal computer mail-order retailers quickly assemble the machine you want with the software you want and deliver it by FedEx or UPS.

target products and services to individual customers and to enable customer services staff to greet customers not as abstractions or strangers but as individuals whose preferences and service history are known to the company.

The process improvement movements—total quality management, business process reengineering, and everything in between—have made customer "something" the driver of process innovation. Initially, it was customer satisfaction: meeting, and thus satisfying, customer expectations. As it has shifted to exceeding expectations by meeting promised levels of service and quality, terms such as customer "delight" and customer "intimacy" have crept into the management vocabulary.

The aim of mass customization is to communicate to customers a sense of genuine familiarity and a willingness, indeed, readiness, to extract from standardized production or delivery mechanisms products or services tailored to the specific wants of individual customers. To achieve it requires more than intent. Commitment must be backed by the capacity to apply mass production techniques to the customization of products or services and information sufficient to define precisely the requisite variants thereon.

Moment of Truth Jan Carlzon, the charismatic former president and CEO of the Scandinavian Airlines System (SAS), coined the term "moment of truth" to describe the key instance of contact between an SAS passenger and a front-line employee that influences the passenger's perception of the airline from that crucial moment onward. For each flight, the typical passenger interacts for fifteen seconds of time with each of five SAS employees, each occasion constituting a moment of truth. It is the combined moments of truth experienced by all of SAS's passengers that both mark SAS's success or failure as a company and that secure competitive advantage.

Of particular import are those instances when the passenger's satisfaction may be in jeopardy, such as when a meal choice is unavailable or a flight is overbooked and the passenger may lose

Have you ever arrived at an airport during rush hour needing to return your rental car just twenty minutes before your plane is scheduled to depart? That's a moment of truth for the rental company, and the company's response to it will stay in your mind for a long time. Avis now puts information at the moment of truth through supplying its staff with handheld devices that access its computers over wireless telecommunications. You are checked in at the car itself, sometimes even before you've unloaded your baggage from it.

his or her seat. Now is when the front-line employee must act instantly on the passenger's behalf, not merely apologizing and smoothing things over, but actually solving the problem on the spot. Carlzon's strategy for ensuring that no golden moment was lost was to give his employees the authority to make those quick decisions. And the strategy worked. SAS became renowned for its exemplary customer service.

During the early 1980s, when Carlzon turned around the ailing airline, information technology was in a rudimentary state by today's standards, with very few personal computers in use and telecommunications being expensive and slow. Today, one can see the obvious extension to the need for putting authority where the moment of truth is: put information there, too.

Negative Working Capital   Negative working capital—understood to mean the bare minimum in raw materials, work-in-process or finished goods inventories, accounts receivable, and uninvested cash and a concomitant reduction of the "asset" side of the balance sheet—is an emerging target of opportunity for firms that have embraced just-in-time business processes. JIT transforms inventory from an asset to a liability. When a product life cycle is as short as 90 days (as it is for Panasonic's television sets), 120 days' worth of inventory will translate into retailer discounts. Using point-of-sale links to the head office, a process-skilled retailer can match shelf replenishment to sales patterns on a daily basis and order as needed via electronic data interchange. A process-skilled manufacturer will deploy just-in-time production and shipping to meet those orders promptly. Electronic order placement and payment will eliminate accounts payables and receivables and the attendant consumption of time and paper; automated cash management systems will sweep funds into electronic lock boxes to be moved throughout the world as needed.

Firms that have achieved industry leadership through JIT can move from near to negative working capital by collecting payments immediately via electronic links while delaying as long as

Just-in-time business and modern information technology render many established accounting rules and conventions irrelevant or misleading. Inventory, for example, is not an asset but a liability that signals lack of streamlining of the supply chain. Accounts receivable are a measure of inefficient cash management; cash should be put to work or returned to shareholders. The very best firms aim at minimizing rather than building up inventory, receivables, and unused cash. They want to stretch payables and thereby transform these financial "liabilities" into a business asset.

possible payments to suppliers. This effectively renders the liability side of the balance sheet greater than the asset side. This target of opportunity is available to market leaders that are able, for example, to pressure suppliers for special payment terms or buy on slow credit and sell at point-of-sale for fast cash.

Negative working capital is a distant, but not unattainable, target for perhaps 50 of the Fortune 1000 and a far larger fraction of medium- and smaller-sized firms that are better run than their customers or suppliers in terms of the just-in-time and on-time processes that most affect working capital. Wal-Mart, for example, is so thoroughly streamlined with respect to point-of-sale to order-to-delivery to payment chain that shelf stock replenishment occurs without reordering. Levi-Strauss taps directly into Wal-Mart's point-of-sale–based sales and inventory data bases to determine when, what, and how much to ship. Because Wal-Mart does not pay for the goods until they are sold, it need not carry them as inventory working capital. The system enables Levi-Strauss to fine-tune its own inventory and eliminates the need for warehouses and distribution centers.

Whether negative working capital materializes as a true opportunity or just a neat turn of phrase that provides a useful way to think about distribution, production, and financial management processes, it points to some new business realities that demand fresh thinking.

- Inventory no longer represents an asset but rather wasted time and resources.

- Powerful customers can insist on process-based partnerships with key suppliers and drop those that cannot comply. (Levi-Strauss's LeviLink electronic data interchange system, which represents the business and technical state-of-the-art, enables it to interact with Wal-Mart in a way that few other suppliers can.)

- The business processes most relevant to creating negative working capital must be viewed in broader terms than a firm's own operations. Firms such as Wal-Mart are building what is sometimes termed the extended enterprise, wherein traditional boundaries between customer and supplier are dissolved. To be locked out of being part of customers' and suppliers' extended enterprises is to be locked out of business.

Network   A network is a web of contacts. Until recently, that web was social or organizational or occasionally a mix; we talk, for instance, about the alumni network of a university, a "club" of managers in a corporation with some shared connections, and the informal networks created by women and minorities in business. Now, used frequently in the plural, networks has also come to mean the telecommunications systems that facilitate new social and organizational webs. As tools for business process investment and innovation, the social and organizational aspects of networks relate primarily to team building and collaboration, the technical aspects to location- and time-independent communication.

Together, the ethos of teams and the technology of telecommunications create entirely new "worknets" of people networks plus technology networks accomplishing what neither alone can do. A social network without telecommunications can engage only in limited communication; when offices in Tokyo are open, offices in New York City are closed and vice versa. But via a telecommunications network that carries electronic mail messages, both offices are always open, allowing parties to carry on conversations in which each receives messages at any time and at any place. Similarly, a face-to-face meeting involving three colleagues located in Missouri, California, and Florida is easy with videoconferencing. The explosive and continuing growth of the use of the Internet to create new social networks via electronic mail, bulletin boards, and shared information resources is further testament to the value-added that networks provide.

The technology of telecommunications enables many forms of worknets but does not generate them. Telecommunications

Telecommunications networks are beginning to make it easier to communicate than not to communicate. That constitutes a major shift. Hierarchy, bureaucracy, and departmental fiefdoms once limited collaboration to individual networks of people. Now, the goal is the team-based, cross-functional, flexible organization in which everyone collaborates as needed.

networks are basically directories of devices and people that can contact one another, in exactly the same manner as your local phone directory of numbers enables you to contact people listed in it. Just like the phone directory, though, the network itself does not constitute communication. You can give someone a phone number to call for help or advice, but if he or she does not use it, the telecommunications network does not generate the social network of help.

Networks, separately and in conjunction with one another, are among the most powerful forces for process innovation. As enablers of teams, collaboration, and time- and location-independent customer service and organization—major elements of the organizational models for the future—networks are of vital import to managers today. Every manager interested in process innovation needs to be familiar with the opportunities of telecommunications, just as every technical professional interested in telecommunications, groupware, and the virtual corporation needs to be familiar with teams, collaboration, and the people side of networks.

See also Case Manager; Client/Server Computing; Collaborate; Coordination Costs; Front-Ending; Groupware; Learning Organization; Lotus Notes; Process Consulting; Worknet; Workstation

Outsource Outsourcing refers to long-term contractual agreements that transfer a previously internal process or set of operations to another company. Firms outsource for a variety of reasons: to accommodate a decision to downsize or focus exclusively on a core business; to eliminate activities that consume time and attention but do not generate competitive advantage; or to exploit special expertise or cost advantages that reflect providers' specialization or economies of scale.

Opinions vary about the value of outsourcing, particularly in the area of information services operations, including systems development, data center operations, and telecommunications services management. The main driver of IT outsourcing has been cost savings, yet anticipated savings may not actually occur.

Outsourcing is a somewhat misleading term, being too often viewed as an either-or alternative to in-house operations. The broader issue is the multisourcing of the entire portfolio of business processes—through joint ventures, customer-supplier collaboration, and outsourcing where that is likely to accrue economic value-added—to enable a firm to focus its attention, resources, and management priorities on a crucial subset. There's nothing new about outsourcing. For decades firms have outsourced employee cafeterias, security, and office cleaning. What is new is the notion that more "strategic" processes might be candidates for outsourcing.

Is it reasonable to expect that an outside company can handle a firm's processes and facilities more economically while adding on its own profit margin? Moreover, many outsourcers offer initial low prices to gain market share but adjust the outsourcing contract, at extra cost, in response to changes in business needs, volumes, locations, and technology.

A far better justification for outsourcing is to focus the attention, resources, and skills of management on processes that are central to the firm's success and on the firm's distinctive competencies. The Business Process Investment framework provides a useful general principle for outsourcing: consider outsourcing those processes that, for your firm, are background liabilities to a firm for which they are identity asset processes.

Thus, for British Petroleum's giant oil exploration unit, the operation of computer data centers is a necessary and expensive background process. So, too, are management accounting and tax compliance. No matter how well BP carries out these activities, they will consume capital without generating economic value-added. The firm's strategic success comes, instead, from its identity processes of searching for promising fields to explore and its priority processes of geological analysis and drilling. By contrast, running data centers constitutes identity and asset processes for the three large computer facilities management companies to which BP outsourced computing, as are management accounting and tax reporting to Arthur Andersen, the leading Big Six accounting firm to which BP outsourced these processes.

There is nothing new about outsourcing per se; all large firms have for decades routinely outsourced many functions, ranging from cafeteria management to computer operations to executive recruitment. What is new is the emphasis on outsourcing more elements of computer and telecommunications operations, which have historically been handled in-house, and the treatment of outsourcing as an element of business *strategy.*

The term "multisourcing" captures this last trend, viewing strategy increasingly as an issue of sourcing, with options being to keep the function in-house, outsource it entirely, work in partnership with a key supplier, work in partnership with key customers, and work with a cooperative industry consortium.

See also Core Process; Identity Processes; Mandated Processes; Partnerships and Alliances

Pareto Chart   A Pareto chart is a bar graph that is used to systematically analyze the causes of quality defects so as to focus resources where they will have the greatest impact.

Consider the following figure. An insurance company breaks out 400 customer complaints thus: 183 (46%) relate to unclear information about coverage; 121 (30%) relate to delays and errors; and the remaining 94 (24%) are distributed among six other

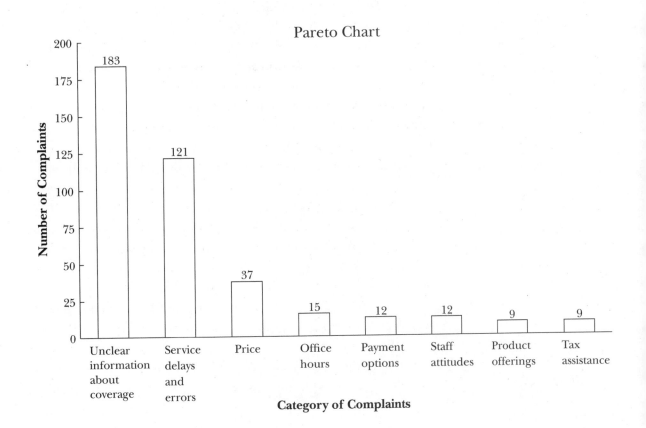

Pareto Chart

The 80-20 rule is one of the most reliable guidelines to rapid prioritization and implementation. You can't be all things to all customers in all markets, can't meet all demands for information systems features, can't solve all problems. So identify the 20 percent of customers that matter most (by providing 80% of your profits) the 80 percent of the system features that matter most (and incur just 20% of the cost), and the 20 percent of problems that are 80 percent of the answer. Ruthless prioritization is essential in a context of rapid, persistent change, downsizing and corresponding growth of workloads, and a surfeit of change initiatives. When everything is a priority, nothing is. The Pareto principle helps prioritize priorities.

categories. Clearly it is in the company's best interest to tackle the first two categories first.

See also Pareto Principle

Pareto Principle   Originally defined by a nineteenth-century economist, the Pareto principle remains one of the most useful rules of thumb in just about every area of business. Often stated as the 80-20 rule, it posits that one gets 80 percent of what one wants for 20 percent of the cost or effort. The question follows: Is it worth expending the extra 80 percent (of dollars or effort) to garner the remaining 20 percent? Variants of the 80-20 rule include: 80 percent of problems are accounted for by 20 percent of causes; 80 percent of profits derive from 20 percent of customers; and 80 percent of warranty claims are generated by 20 percent of the product portfolio.

See also Pareto Chart

Partnerships and Alliances   Partnerships and alliances are formal or informal arrangements that firms make with each other to help manage the complexity of business without having to rely solely on internal resources. The terms are nearly interchangeable, with "partnerships" implying more formal mutual commitments than characterize "alliances"; "consortia" and "joint ventures" refer to similar agreements. All of these arrangements may—indeed, frequently do—bring competitors together. Walter Wriston, former chairman of Citibank, described the role of partnerships in creating the infrastructures of international "borderless" banking as "Cooperate in the morning, compete in the afternoon."

When companies decide to reengineer or focus their business processes, they typically downsize and outsource many functions. Some then want to augment their capabilities, especially for processes demanding a mix of skills and resources that benefit from specialization, by building close and long-term relationships with other firms as partners. Thus, for instance, a consumer foods company spending hundreds of millions of dollars on information technology may seek a partnership relation with its primary hardware and software vendor, drawing on the vendor's expertise in systems development processes.

Others look for complementary capabilities. Glaxo, the world's number two pharmaceutical firm, began its rise from the middle of the pack when it entered into an alliance with Hoffman Laroche whereby Laroche's sales force sold Glaxo's Xantac (the first drug to reach sales of a billion dollars a year). Glaxo possessed strong marketing and research processes but lacked scale and skill in distribution and sales processes; Hoffman Laroche had lacked product to sell. Both parties, then, gained from the alliance, even while remaining competitors.

Some partnerships are created in order to share resources and gain advantages of scale or speed. After a decade of often hostile competition, for example, Apple and IBM formed a partnership, along with Motorola, to develop a new generation of computer chips, the Power PC, and make a leap ahead of Intel, whose chips dominate the market. Similarly, Apple and IBM, in a massive effort to displace Microsoft, made a partnership to create a generation of computer operating systems.

Partnership is between equals, with each party frankly expressing its own interests in open negotiations and working toward a "sum-sum" or win-win situation. The notion of partnership flies in the face of traditional competitive relationships, which are based on zero-sum situations (meaning "one of us wins, the other loses"). Thus, whereas retailers have long guarded closely information about their suppliers' sales patterns in their stores, hoping to use it as an edge in contract negotiations, Wal-Mart now allows Levi-Strauss to tap directly into its point-of-sale databases, stocking the shelves without Wal-Mart's placing any orders. Texas Instruments similarly shares information with its telecommunications providers about their reliability and service, and Xerox gives its suppliers direct access to data that show its assessments of their quality.

This level of relationship rests on trust and openness. Many firms' corporate cultures, grounded in secrecy and wariness of cooperating with "outsiders," impede such trusts and tacitly encourage mutual suspicion among competitors asked to cooperate. Such is the situation in many alliances between manufacturers to share the development costs of a technology, gain joint advantages in distribution, or license products.

Partnership is easy to announce, tough to effect, as these not atypical cases illustrate.

- Galileo is a consortium of airlines formed to create a new generation of reservations systems intended to ward off American Airlines' dominance of the industry through its Sabre system. The senior representative to Galileo of one of Europe's two largest airlines was excluded from all of that airline's strategic planning meetings and informed by the head of marketing, "We may have 25 percent of Galileo, but we don't want anyone in X and Y [two other leading airlines involved in the Galileo alliance] knowing what we're up to. As far as I'm concerned, you're part of the competition now."

- The senior executive in charge of distribution in a large foods company opposed working with a leading customer on electronic data interchange links between the two firms, saying, "ABC [its main competitor] isn't the enemy—Z [the customer] is." The customer as competitor is an interesting slant on business.

- One of the largest vendors in the computer field made partnership with its customers a priority in the late 1980s but was very wary about providing them with information on its product and pricing plans. As one customer commented, "They want to know our seven-year business plan but clam up when we want to know about theirs;

they tell us they can't do this because of their
competition finding out."

Partnerships and alliances are a growing part of business.
They allow firms to focus their capabilities, manage complexity,
and gain many process advantages through drawing on complementary skills and resources. They also can transform customer
relationships in development and service. When Boeing brought
its airline customers into the development process for the 767
aircraft, it took time for both parties to become comfortable with
each other, but the payoff for both was huge: Boeing increased
its speed to market, quality of development, and customer satisfaction, and the airlines influenced the design details to get
exactly the plane they wanted.

In outsourcing, alliances, partnerships, and joint ventures,
firms must first ask what is the basis for mutual trust. They then
need to look at their own cultural and reward processes as opportunities or necessities for process investment, including even radical reengineering of them. Trust is the new currency of business.
Ours is an era of growing customer-supplier, supplier-supplier,
and competitor-competitor cooperation as a driver of change and
innovation. That makes trust as a capability—the organizational
capability for trust and the credibility and track record to be
trusted—a source of competitive advantage.

See also Outsource; Shamrock Organization; Trust

Penzias Axiom   Arno A. Penzias, a Nobel prize winner for phys-
ics (1978) who also wrote an influential book on information and
the economy, makes a powerful point that we call the Penzias
axiom: any person who or step that stands between a customer
and a computer that can *completely* fulfill the customer's request
will eventually be removed. The bank teller who used to input the
information about your transaction into a computer is being
superseded by an ATM. Administrative and mailroom staff who
once generated, transported, received, and processed floods of

purchase orders, invoices, and payments are now increasingly bypassed as information and money move directly from computer to computer via electronic data interchange.

Of course, there are many situations in which the people standing between the computer and customer add some value. Most of us still make travel plans through travel agents rather than key our flight, hotel, rental car, and entertainment reservations into a personal computer. To date, the PC does not fully meet our needs for simplicity of service, advice, and searching out special deals. But the Penzias axiom implies a relentless, almost remorseless, march of change that will, over time, eliminate a large number of jobs in the quest to improve customer service.

What happens to the jobs and people displaced as the outcome of axiom? By definition, the jobs are not value-adding to the customer or the company, and many of the people in them have no special value-adding skills. Consider a supervisor in the accounts payable department, whose experience is mainly in the very procedures that electronic data interchange displaces. In an economy where more and more firms are displacing jobs, devaluing skills, and aggressively downsizing, he or she has little opportunity to move to another firm.

Already, the evidence is that millions of jobs will disappear. Purchasing departments in large companies typically shrink from several hundred staff to around twenty, twenty being the number needed to handle such value-adding roles as contract negotiation, quality management, supplier relationships, management planning, and so on in an electronic data interchange environment. Estimates show that in the 1990s, the Fortune 1000 firms have eliminated well over a million jobs; the Penzias axiom implies that they will continue for many years to eliminate even more.

Reengineering, downsizing, outsourcing, and many other process improvements and innovations may be driven mainly by the wish to transform customer service and organizational capabilities, but they are job-killers in the long term.

See also Business Process Reengineering; Empowerment; Trust

Plan, Do, Check, Act (P.D.C.A.) "Plan, Do, Check, and Act" is W. E. Deming's recommended base for quality planning. Termed a "wheel" by Deming, it is also known as a Shewhart diagram. An expanded version, construed as a continuous circle, is depicted in the figure below.

The components of the Deming wheel are defined thus.

- Plan: define a unit's mission (ask why it exists and why it *should* exist) and identify its outputs; identify the internal and external customers for, and prioritize, its products or services; identify customer needs *in the customer's language* and translate them into the appropriate business language; establish a formal plan for meeting customers' needs; and designate quality indicators (i.e., list what is to be measured on an ongoing basis).

- Do: implement the plan.

- Check: continuously review quality indicators and return to customers for feedback.

- Act: use results and feedback to improve and replan, that is, spin the wheel again and start over.

Total quality management methods, including the Deming wheel, can seem mechanistic and overstructured. But they use-

The Deming Wheel

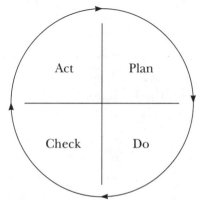

Many firms' top managers climbed onto the TQM bandwagon, made quality an announced priority, and assigned someone to be its advocate, champion, and mover. Too often, the designee was a relatively junior manager with a fancy title, no power or budget, and little influence. Such vice presidents for quality were evangelists in the wilderness, largely ignored by the mainstream of the business; through them firms paid lip service to quality. Will the same gap between the process champion's job title and organizational clout emerge in reengineering and the learning organization? If so, look for the same results: great expectations and aspirations that generate disappointment.

fully convey a central lesson from the winners in the quality race, notably the Japanese firms that applied and validated Deming's work: that there is no substitute for discipline and rigor. Continuous improvement relies on continuous effort. The Plan and Do elements of Deming's wheel correspond to strategy and implementation. Check and Act emphasize follow-up. Feedback, particularly quality control data, spins the wheel.

Process Champion A process champion is a manager who possesses the seniority and organizational clout to champion a cross-functional initiative that transcends established lines of authority and responsibility. The role of champion may be one of informal sponsorship or of more structured advocacy, reflecting top management's recognition of the need to balance flexibility and stability. The matching of formal structure to roles and responsibility to authority is implicit in stability; flexibility frequently destabilizes all.

Process innovation is, almost by definition, cross-functional. Organizing around processes, however desirable, is extraordinarily difficult to achieve in a way that is stable. Even if a major process is made the basis of organization (R&D is the organizational kernel in leading pharmaceutical firms such as Glaxo, brand management processes in fast-moving consumer goods firms such as Procter & Gamble), many other processes will cut across organizational units. Customer service, product development, and marketing, for example, all interact with finance, which comprises investment, cash management, budgeting, reporting, and so forth. Even in a firm driven by research and development or brand management, finance will maintain a separate organizational base and exercise authority outside other process spheres. A process champion is essential to matching process and function. In Glaxo, which left the pack to achieve the highest market value of any British firm and become the number two pharmaceutical firm in the world, finance, even though primarily a support function secondary to research and development processes, is a distinctive and independent corporate resource (i.e., stock price matters, as does raising capital). In firms not led by a dominant process, the finance function remains just a set of functional processes that affects and stands apart from other processes. Only a process champion can ensure finance is embedded in a process and not kept separate as a fiefdom.

Designating relatively junior staff members process owners and expecting them to coordinate across lines of authority is a mistake the total quality movement has frequently made that accounts for the 70 percent of quality management initiatives that reportedly fail. The reengineering movement's more realistic appreciation of the need for top-level authority to harness the forces that drive radical change is reflected in its more frequent use of the term process champion.

Process Consulting   Process consulting, essentially the field of organizational development's application of the behavioral sciences to change management facilitation, and organizational diagnosis, originated in the 1970s. Roughly speaking, process consulting addresses organizational processes, while business process reengineering, quality management, and offshoots of industrial engineering address the content of work processes.

Two very different traditions and cultures are at work here. Process consulting is concerned with the "soft" side of change—people, attitudes, culture, politics, facilitation, and communication—process reengineering with the "hard" side—workflows, process design, metrics, job skills, and technology. At the extremes, process consultants understand people but not business, process reengineers workflows but not people.

The evolution of the total quality management movement in the United States shows the vital need to handle the hard and soft sides of change simultaneously. TQM initially emphasized the hard side; statistical quality control, rigorous standards, discipline, and management by fact are very much mind-over-heart and method-over-people approaches. Many of the quality programs

One expert commentator acerbically argues that the term "reengineering" appeals to computer professionals because it ignores people and embraces the tidy, mechanistic view of the organization they have become most comfortable with. It seems reasonable to talk about reengineering the accounts receivable process. How about reengineering the AR staff? That's dismissive and depersonalizing, and makes people peripheral to workflows. It is very much the flavor of most of the reengineering literature. Process consulting puts people at the center. Managing the dynamics of change through people affords access to a broad, rich body of knowledge and experience. Process consulting, which embodies this knowledge and experience, is the human side of business process innovation that can and should complement the industrial engineer's workflow-oriented side.

that failed during TQM's early years were little more than alternative bureaucracies that prescribed new metrics to which workers were expected to conform. Respect for people gained credence in TQM as managers learned that they did not necessarily know best, that work was frequently most understood by those who did it, and that shared values and rewards in pursuit of a shared goal could unleash a surge of energy. Recent reports of successful TQM programs acknowledge people to be central rather than peripheral. The evolution of business process reengineering will likely follow a similar track. The lip service paid by the reengineering literature to the soft side of process change ignores the many lessons process consultants have learned about mobilizing people, building teams, and helping individuals make change an ally instead of a threat.

Not only must the workflow-related activities that are the focus of reengineering and the people who interact with one another in the execution of those activities not be separated, but the technology that mediates the two must be taken into account. Process consultants are inclined to underplay the nonpeople elements, reengineering proponents the nonworkflow elements. Management must ensure that they do not.

Process Owner   Process owner is the term used to identify the individual who is assigned responsibility for a process and accorded the authority needed to fulfill that responsibility. Authority and accountability for processes, because they are defined in terms of parts of a process—functional area, department, activity—tend to be highly fragmented in most companies. Customer procurement, for example, is initiated by a customer order and progresses through production scheduling, manufacturing operations, distribution, accounts receivables, and finance. Authority and accountability are distributed among the respective functional units. A process owner would exercise responsibility for the customer procurement process end-to-end, employing influence or management authority to ensure its coordination.

The concept of process owner being relatively new, examples in practice are few. What it implies is the matching of authority and accountability in a cross-functional environment. Three practical approaches include (1) assigning process ownership to an individual within the existing functional structure, (2) designating as process owner a senior corporate manager, and (3) organizing around business processes, with the process owner being equivalent to a line executive and vice versa. The first leaves the existing authority-accountability relationship intact and introduces a new role, a type of coordinator who must negotiate with the functional areas. The second approach coopts existing authority by transferring responsibility for a function to an individual who possesses organizational clout and can command, not just negotiate. The third approach supplants functional structure by developing authority and accountability around processes directly.

Each approach can be effective, but experience managing information technology in large organizations suggests some cautions. The corporate IT function is fundamentally cross-functional. Its service role defines its business responsibility, and its oversight role, explicitly or implicitly, defines its authority. The old data processing function exercised considerable authority; it was, in effect, a monopoly with the latitude to dictate procedure to captive business units. Business accountability, on the other hand, was practically nil, a source of continuing frustration for "users" (a designation that relegates business units to a lesser role than clients or colleagues of the IT function). Today, the pendulum has swung; the function is seen increasingly as a business service unit, and decision-making authority over planning priorities and resource allocation has devolved to business units. The diagram below suggests descriptors of the function at the extremes of low and high authority and accountability.

When the function is ceded little authority but held highly accountable, its managers tend to become whipping posts, expected to deliver ever-higher levels of service in the absence of power to ensure effective coordination of infrastructures, cross-functional resource sharing, and avoidance of multitechnology chaos. In the rare instances in which the function is neither granted authority nor held particularly accountable, it serves principally to operate corporate data centers, peripheral to the mainstream of business and to business units' use of IT. It is in this capacity that we refer to the function as an information janitor; with little expected of it and even less latitude to coordinate, it struggles to maintain some semblance of order within the corporate information resource and to clean up after the independent data centers operated by the business units. The function as monopolist has become an endangered species, an evolutionary dead end. The function's future is as information executive, a highly accountable role that possesses the authority to fulfill corporate and business unit expectations.

The descriptors used to characterize the IT function can also be applied to process owners. Conferring the title without a clear statement and metrics for measuring the business achievement is little more than an exercise in public relations, a token effort rather than a serious commitment. If authority remains with the

	AUTHORITY	
	Low	High
Low	Information Janitor	Monopolist
High	Whipping Post	Information Executive

ACCOUNTABILITY

functional unit, a designated process owner will be merely a process janitor. When total quality management became *de rigueur* for businesses a few years ago, many companies assigned junior staff to oversee quality across functions. These "advocates" published newsletters and spoke at conferences on quality, but their role was clearly temporary and evaporated over time. So will the role of process owners who lack ownership rights.

The creation of monopolist process owners is unlikely, but there exist many process monopolies, fiefdoms of administrative units, most often corporate groups, that tyrannize business operations via paper and control of resources. The process movements generally end such monopolies, either by increasing business responsibility, as by reengineering the travel expense, budgeting, or contract approval process, or by relocating authority, as by outsourcing the offending activities or substituting software systems for administrative functionaries.

Assigning process ownership to corporate managers already accorded ample authority and business responsibility effectively finesses many of the problems implicit in the monopolist and whipping post syndromes.

Process Paradox We characterize as "the process paradox" the circumstance of impressive benefits created by process innovation failing to generate value for a firm. General Motors and IBM, while both are Baldrige Award winners for quality management, are good examples of the process paradox. Study after study documents improvements on the order of 40 to 80 percent in the cost, cycle time, or reliability of business processes that yield no concomitant improvement in the economic performance of the associated business units.

We suggested in the Introduction that the paradox reflects the difference between getting a process right and getting the right process right, where "right" refers to some aspect of the link between a process and the factors that most affect a firm's business and organizational health. The industrial engineering tradition

Mutual Benefit brilliantly reengineered its insurance policy issuing processes and filed for Chapter 11 bankruptcy protection. IBM and GM won the Baldrige Award for manufacturing quality at a time when their leadership, product launch, marketing, and customer service processes were pushing the firms into a black hole. Successful reengineering projects that generate striking benefits rarely generate improvements in overall business unit performance. That's the process paradox—great benefits, no added value. Resolving the paradox is a matter of focusing on which process to get right.

that underlies much of total quality management and most of business process reengineering tends to zero in on processes with well-defined workflows and eliminate attendant waste. Of greatest relevance here are what are termed "salience" and "worth" in the Business Process Investment framework. Salience is the importance of a process relative to a firm's strategic identity and priorities, worth, the economic nature of the process (i.e., whether it is an asset that generates economic value-added or a liability that drains value, no matter how well executed).

The process paradox is a warning signal to managers, a reminder that process innovation is a strategic and economic issue first, and that workflow improvement becomes significant only when management has correctly identified which process to get right.

See also Worth/Salience Matrix

Process Predator   We use the term process predator to describe a company that exploits its business process capabilities and insights to intrude on firms outside its industry. Process predators often have the advantage of no investment in the traditional players' expensive process infrastructures and are able to bypass these with prohibitively expensive to duplicate information technologies of their own. A successful predator initiative will frequently leave the prey years behind given the long lead times required to develop a comprehensive IT platform.

A few process predators and their prey will serve to illustrate.

- British Airways wrested from Marriott Hotels control of the latter's own product in international markets. The airline recognized that travelers rarely make international hotel reservations before their flight reservations, that it had in place one of the most powerful and comprehensive computerized reservation systems in the world, and that it would cost little to add hotels to this infrastructure. Moreover, the service was a natural extension of its mainstream reservation processes

("You're confirmed on BA Flight 123. May I help you with a hotel?"). A consortium that contracted with American Airlines to create a catch-up system made information technology history with what amounted to perhaps *the* most expensive IT debacle. Late to begin with, and then found to be crawling with "bugs," the more than half-a-billion-dollar system was abandoned. The process predator is still feeding on the prey.

- Fidelity Investments (securities) and USAA (insurance) command large numbers of loyal customers for whom they provide banking products conveniently over the phone. Such is the level of their customer service that they are effectively better banks than most banks.

- Dell Computer, perhaps the epitome of the process predator, redefined the personal computer retailing industry through telephone sales, customized product assembly, and UPS package delivery, in the process, transforming retail stores from assets to liabilities.

Customers are indifferent to industry boundaries. They are unlikely to reject a British Airways reservations agent's offer to make their hotel reservations. Customers want value; process predators provide it.

Process predators are in a sense the new business strategists of the information era. Almost by definition not locked into old mindsets about industry and core industry processes, their view of process tends to be broader than that of their prey.

Managers who wish to preserve their companies from predation need to consider seriously the following questions.

- What do our customers get when they contact us? What else might they like, if offered?

- Who offers it today?

- Why can't we?

- Why shouldn't we?

The most dangerous competitors are increasingly the outsiders that, lacking the advantage of an existing process infrastructure, bring to bear a new one that transforms the "advantage" of the old into a millstone. Britain's First Direct captured 10 percent of the national car insurance market in two years doing business entirely by phone and mail. The opportunity had existed for a decade, but the traditional players had no incentive to attack their established process base.

- What would be the cost of providing it?

- What are the costs of the existing providers?

- What sort of start-up firm might be able to provide it more conveniently and inexpensively?

- If provision is not by "us," but by "them," are we in danger of becoming process prey? Who might the predator be?

They must also not lose sight of the fact that business processes do not inherently belong to any particular industry.

Process Redesign   *See* Business Process Reengineering

Process as Capital   Processes are more than just workflows; they comprise a substantial component of the capital invested by a company for the long term. That capital is either a financial asset that generates economic value-added or a deficit that drains value from the firm. Bennett Stewart tersely defines capital as "an approximation of the economic book value of all cash invested in going-concern business activities" (*The Quest for Value* [New York: HarperBusiness, 1991], 744). That's an investor's perspective, and it should be a manager's as well. It is not, however, an accountant's perspective, and, to their companies' detriment, many managers focus only on the assets that appear on the accounting balance sheet.

The rules of financial accounting clearly specify what may be treated as an asset for tax and public reporting of income statements and balance sheets. Those rules exclude research and development, even when R&D is the foundation of the firm's current capabilities and its future growth. Merck and Intel, for instance, became and remain leaders in their industry through their R&D processes, which they consider identity assets. But accounting and tax rules treat them as an expense, an annual cost rather than a long-term investment. If the two firms were to cut their R&D in half, their profits would soar while their business advantage would decline, a contradiction between the rules of accounting and taxation and the logic of business investment.

There are many other instances of this contradiction. Software development is expensed, even though a large firm may have spent around $2 billion on the software assets in use that are major competitive long-term assets, such as American Airlines' Sabre and Wal-Mart's point-of-sale systems. Motorola's much-admired investment in education as a cornerstone of its long-term growth and innovation is also a cost that reduces profits, but the physical facilities of Motorola "U" are an asset on the balance sheet. The managers of American Airlines, Wal-Mart, Motorola, Merck, and Intel manage those nontangible assets as such, and investors value them as assets.

Processes are not handled as assets by the tax and accounting system, either, but logically should be by the management system. Process capital is the approximate value of all cash invested in a process, including recruitment, training, software development, maintenance and operations, facilities, and many other costs. These elements are integral parts of the process asset, regardless of accounting rules. They may be integral parts of a process liability, too, and thus drain economic value. Administrative processes are a typical example. Consider, for instance, employee expense reporting. Is this just a minor expense or does it tie up substantial capital? The accounting system is unlikely to answer the question. It won't show the capital invested in the requisite software, computers, and departmental telecommunications networks, especially the costs of maintaining and updating them and providing the technical staff support that typically exceeds the costs of acquisition and development. It won't show the capital tied up by the facilities, supplies, and services used by the central financial unit handling the process; recruitment and training; or ongoing and unavoidable annual costs of management time, business unit personnel, facilities, and so on. This capital is scattered across many budgets and accounts and across many years of expensing the costs.

A primary insight of the business process reengineering movement is that business processes need to be viewed end-to-end across functional and departmental boundaries. The functional organization blocks this view. Add to this the insight of the Business Process Investment framework—that business processes need to be viewed in terms of end-to-end economics across budget and accounts as well—and you have a base for knowing exactly which processes tie up capital. These processes are thus targets of opportunity for increasing the value from the capital and for focusing your firm's reengineering efforts on the processes that most directly affect business positioning and shareholder value.

See also Economic Value-Added; Shareholder Value; Worth/ Salience Matrix

Quality Control   Quality control and quality assurance are interchangeable terms that refer to sets of disciplined activities aimed at ensuring high levels of quality in a service or product. "Discipline" is the key element. Quality management is in many ways the organizational equivalent of a total reformation in personal habits: dieting, sticking with an exercise plan, pursuing target goals, and striving to meet commitments. Old habits are harsh taskmasters, more so to organizations. Sincerity cannot substitute for technique. Quality control must have a basis in specific, *measurable* targets and acceptable limits for variation in quality-related characteristics of products and services.

Quality control at its worst is a new metrics bureaucracy that views numbers as ends in themselves. At its best, it assures universal acceptance of and commitment to clearly defined and well-understood measures of performance.

Quality Function Deployment (QFD)   Quality function deployment (QFD) refers to a set of tools the use of which is intended to ensure that product and service design are from the outset driven by customer requirements. The idea is to consider customer satisfaction with respect to such "downstream" processes as support, procurement, marketing, and after-sales service before design engineering, production, and other "upstream" processes are completed.

Widely deployed by Japanese manufacturing companies, QFD attempts to reverse the historical separation of engineering, production, and sales and marketing that results in product features being developed without a nod to broader business and organizational realities. The tradition of separation presumes that "elegant" solutions that conform to technical specifications will satisfy customers. Units closer to customers are likely to be aware of, but unable to influence, clarity of marketing message, product or service explanation and ease of use, and convenience or ease of repair. QFD tools such as the House of Quality matrix provide a discipline base for migrating from the "throw it over the wall" mentality to cross-functional teams that work together from design to delivery. The underlying insight that QFD imparts—that quality is defined not by a product or service but by a customer's relationship to it—is heeded when the product development process is expanded to include all functions and processes involved in that relationship.

See House of Quality

Reengineering   *See* Business Process Reengineering

Self-Source   Self-sourcing describes the transfer of process execution from supplier to customer, to their mutual advantage. A salad bar is a self-sourcing arrangement. A manager who uses a portable computer in lieu of the company's graphics department to generate presentation graphs is self-sourcing. Self-sourcing banking services through ATMs reduces bank processing costs by approximately 35 percent (relative to the cost of human tellers) and virtually eliminates errors in the bargain, while affording customers heretofore undreamed convenience, flexibility, and autonomy.

Self-sourcing is an illustration of what Business Process Invest-

Do-it-yourself can cut the cost of providing a service and simultaneously increase customer satisfaction. Examples range from automated credit card account inquiry systems accessed by telephone to self-service salad bars. One self-sourcing move that signals a major shift in the basics of international banking is Hong Kong Shanghai Banking Corporation's Hexagon system, which enables corporate customers to handle their own foreign exchange (FX) and trade finance transactions, as well as conventional cash management, via more than 45,000 on-line computer terminals in thirty-five countries. FX used to be handled entirely by banks, a number of which actively blocked efforts by multinationals to bypass them.

ment terms the Penzias axiom, for Nobel prize laureate and author Arno Penzias, whose insightful book on the new role of information in business and society conveys a profound insight—that persons or steps interposed between customers and computer systems that can *fully* meet their needs will, in time, be eliminated. Thus bank tellers are made redundant by ATM technology, order-inventory and payables personnel by electric data interchange systems, and customer-service staff by touchtone telephone-accessible automated inquiry systems. The essence of self-sourcing is providers creating the wherewithal for customers to participate in the improvement of services by assuming responsibility for some part of their delivery.

Shamrock Organization   British theorist Charles Handy, who sees tomorrows' organizations being highly disaggregated, suggested the term shamrock organization for the practical conception of a process-centered organizational form (depicted in the diagram below) that is likely to increasingly replace the traditional hierarchical pyramid.

The small, central group of managers and professional, including technical, staff at the core of the shamrock reflects the firm's core competencies, that is, its distinctive skill base and strategic resources. It is here, at the center, that a business's operations and forward planning are coordinated. The three leaves that connect to the center, but not to one another, represent:

- operating units (the only area for full-time employment);
- strategic (as contrasted with commodity) suppliers and individuals or companies contracted to perform all nonessential work;
- the part-time and temporary employees (the fastest growing, and soon perhaps largest, segment of the labor force) and home-based professionals and contractors whose specialized skills and services are utilized as needed.

The logic of the shamrock organization is to keep the "head office" small and focused and drastically cut staff numbers and costs by outsourcing as much as possible. Intended when he proposed it to provoke what Handy calls "upside-down thinking," today the shamrock organization doesn't look at all futuristic. Few large companies have not made some effort to trim their size. Typical of these efforts are the elimination of large numbers of middle managers and redeployment of functions from the center closer to the customer (usually by exploiting some information technology or other). The consumer foods company Unilever, for example, although larger than Procter & Gamble, has a head

A small core of full-time managers and professionals at the center of the firm; a group of increasingly autonomous, flexible, and lean business units; tight relationships with strategic customers, suppliers, and business partners; and contracting on an as-needed, when-needed basis with contractors and temps—that's the most likely shape of the organization of tomorrow. Why? Because these are the principal trends today.

The Shamrock Organization

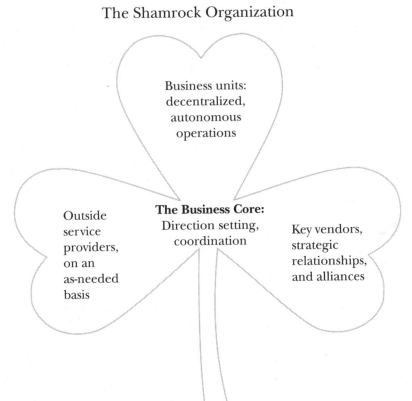

Business units: decentralized, autonomous operations

The Business Core: Direction setting, coordination

Outside service providers, on an as-needed basis

Key vendors, strategic relationships, and alliances

Source: Charles Handy, *The Age of Unreason* (Boston: Harvard Business School Press, 1990).

office of about only one hundred full-time employees. AT&T and IBM, neither of which are historical paragons of flexibility, have stripped their sales forces of permanent offices and provided them with technologies that enable them to work from their homes and automobiles. Outsourcing as a way to greatly reduce staff has become trendy among U.S. firms, as has replacing full-time staff with lower paid part-time workers.

Say the shamrock *is* the likely blueprint for tomorrow's organizations. What are its implications for successful and sustained process improvement? Is, for example, size a factor for the companies that possess the best process capabilities in a business sector or have most effectively exploited information technology to improve service delivery or coordination? That is, what is the lower limit of size for the center of the shamrock and operating units?

In the absence of formal study, wide reading suggests to the authors that were the best of the best to become the standard, the entire economy could be run with 10 percent of today's labor force. Verifone, which produces nearly all in-store credit card authorization devices, earned revenues of $150 million with no head office, no secretaries, and, for the most part, no offices or staff. Rosenbluth Travel, with sales of well over a billion dollars, employs only 2,500 people. Fidelity Investment's handful of staff provide full-service banking with no branches. That firms can accommodate greatly increased volumes and deliver better service with fewer employees is clearly evident in the process improvements discussed in the Introduction. Recall Telcot's increased productivity—from 9,000 to 450,000 transactions per employee, per year—and Taco Bell's elimination of 75 percent of its store supervisors. Consider, too, the almost routine reductions in staff of 40 percent or more reported by reengineering studies and it becomes very clear that the process-driven firm of 2005 will be quite small at its center.

Implicit in the shamrock model are the principles and findings of many of the process movements. The bases for operations in the virtual corporation are alliances and outsourcing. The learning organization emphasizes education and collaboration. Its emphasis on radically pruning process steps and, as a consequence, people, has led many to equate reengineering with layoffs.

For full-time employees at the center of the shamrock and in the operating units and for outsourcing providers and contractors, the process-driven firm of 2005 is a bright prospect; it is a bleak prospect for part-time workers and staff who have been, and will be, laid off as a consequence of process improvements.

Shareholder Value Shareholder value is the total return on invested capital that accrues to the owners of a company's stock. "Shareholder" here does not refer to Wall Street traders but to the wide range of investors who provide the long-term capital that is the entire basis for building and sustaining a successful firm; these include most employees in pension funds (55% of all large companies' stock is invested here), mutual funds, and many other forms of saving.

Shareholder value is increasingly recognized in both financial theory and successful management practice as the most meaningful target for and measure of business performance. Regardless of apparent profitability, reported earnings per share, and income statement, a firm that generates an after-tax cash flow that exceeds its cost of capital will thrive and one that does not will falter.

Many successful firms lose their competitive position by unwittingly wasting capital. They raise capital easily, invest it in profitable projects, and report growing earnings. But savvy investors, who in the longer term set the market, are not fooled by the earnings picture. They know, and studies corroborate, that there is no correlation between earnings and stock price but that there is a very strong correlation between economic value-added and market value-added. Economic value-added is the after-tax cash flow generated by the company's operations minus the cost of all the capital the company has used to generate that cash flow. Cost of capital is the weighted average of interest on loans plus the cost of equity. The riskier or weaker the company, the higher its cost of capital; banks charge higher interest on its loans, bond-

Fifty-five percent of large companies' stock is invested in pension funds. Add to this individuals' holdings in mutual funds, employee stock options, and universities' endowments that fund a large fraction of tuition costs, and it becomes clear that "shareholders" are not just anonymous Wall Street money managers. Shareholders are most of us.

holders require a higher rate of return, and shareholders are unwilling to pay a premium for its stock.

Economic value-added determines the increase in shareholder value generated by the firm; this market value-added is the increase in the market value of the firm, that is, the premium investors will pay for the stock. If investors see economic value-added growing, they bid the stock up. If not, they bid it down. The correlation, shown below, along with a comparable graph plotting the lack of relationship between earnings per share and stock price, is very strong.

It is easy to explain in commonsense terms why shareholder value carries more significance than earnings per share. We handle (or should) our personal affairs with shareholder value in mind. For ourselves, shareholder value is directly equivalent to net worth, and economic value-added to after-tax cash flow. We don't try to maximize the equivalent of profit. To do so would mean trying to state as high a gross taxable income on our federal and state tax statements as we could. Instead, we try to reduce tax, maximizing deductions and pushing income into next year, rather than taking it now, thereby increasing our after-tax cash flow. We also pay attention to the cost of borrowing. If we rent out an $80,000 house, we calculate the after-tax return. Our gross profit is the rent minus operating costs. From that profit we deduct the mortgage interest, which is our cost of capital for the $80,000 asset that generates the income. That cost is tax deductible, so even if the rental shows a loss the deduction adds after-tax cash flow to our savings, which represents the equivalent of economic value-added and increase in net worth.

Cost of capital and after-tax cash flow are the main elements of net worth, as they are of shareholder value. Imagine a situation in which certificates of deposit are earning 5.5 percent interest. A friend boasts to you that he is getting a guaranteed return of 11.8 percent and has deposited $28,000 in this instrument. Are you impressed? Probably so, until you casually ask your friend how he got the $28,000 to invest. "Oh, I borrowed on all my credit cards."

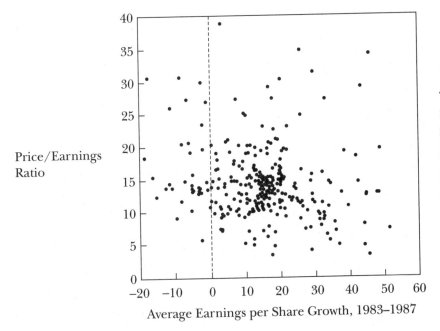

This graph shows
no relationship between
growth in earnings and
price/earnings ratio.
The same is true for
many variants: earnings
are not correlated with
market value.

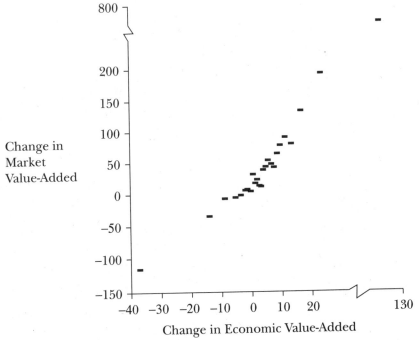

This graph shows a
very strong correlation
between economic
value-added and
shareholder value
(market value-added).
It plots 1,000 companies
in groups of 25.

Source: The Quest for Value by G. Bennett Stewart. Copyright © by Ballinger Publishing Company.
Reprinted by permission of HarperCollins Publishers, Inc.

Given that the interest rate on his cards runs at 15 to 18 percent, the 11.8 percent return is not at all the deal it appears to be. Your friend is outperforming the market but draining his net worth.

Companies make the equivalent of this mistake. Here are just a few representative examples.

- In 1992, Spiegel, the catalog retailer, reported a net profit of $119 million. Its total capital was $1.6 billion, and the cost of capital was 11.1 percent (a weighted average of debt at 6.8% and equity at 18.3%). The carrying cost of this capital was thus $1.6 billion × 11.1 percent: $178 million. Even though it is profitable, the firm is actually draining shareholder value. With ten years of such profits, a firm will go broke.

- In the late 1980s, the managers of RJR, the tobacco company, underwent what one commentator calls an "earnings addiction." For example, at the end of 1988, RJR offered its distributors incentives to stock up on inventory, thereby greatly increasing sales and reported profits. The stocking up, however, produced overstock; the distributors had accumulated close to 20 billion unsold cigarettes when RJR announced its next semiannual price increase. It had sold the cigarettes at a lower price and had paid excise duty earlier than it needed to. Shipments dropped 29 percent and 17 percent in the next quarters. *Yet the stock price went up.* The smart investors who drive the market saw management at last facing up to the situation and taking action to restore the firm's economic health. The stock price of the "profitable" RJR had been $55; the less profitable firm was taken private at $110 a share. Bennett Stewart, whose book *The Quest for Value* is a superb analysis of economic value-added and its direct link to shareholder value, comments on RJR, "Kick the earnings habit. Join the cash-flow generation."

- In the 1960s, W.T. Grant grew its earnings into bankruptcy. It implemented an aggressive sales policy and a strategy of store expansion. Sales and profits grew at an impressive rate, but inventories and credit card receivables grew much faster. From 1968 to 1975, its most profitable years, Grant's economic value-added was negative, despite the earnings growth. W.T. Grant is no longer in business.

Cash flow generated by the efficient use of capital is now the mainstream of corporate financial strategy and investment strategy. Legendary maestro investor Warren Buffett speaks of "owners' earnings" and the finance theorists focus on "free cash flow"; the many companies that have adopted this perspective generally use economic value-added as the new management metric. Firms such as CSX, PepsiCo, AT&T, and Quaker report that it provides a discipline for planning and a measure of management performance that has significantly improved corporate performance, mainly because it focuses management's attention on the use of all capital.

Processes are capital, not just workflows, so all decisions about them must be based on increasing shareholder value as the investment metric. The process paradox—that substantial benefits from process improvement so often do not lead to improved business performance—reflects the widespread lack of attention in the process movements to the capital nature of processes.

See also Economic Value-Added

Six Sigma Quality Six sigma quality refers to a target set and achieved by Motorola, namely: 3.4 defects per million "opportunities" for a defect to occur (each additional component or process step adds an opportunity). Technically, six sigma is defined as six standard deviations from the average for a measure. Applied to the measurement of quality, it means that 99.99997 percent of products meet the target. Motorola set its seemingly impossibly difficult-to-meet target after having *already* improved quality by a

Motorola's manufacturing process admits almost no product defects. It took fifteen years for this best of the best firm to establish six sigma quality as an attainable standard for other firms. There's no "quality tooth fairy" that will leave total quality under the CEO's pillow. The time needed to transform an organization appears to be in the range of ten to fifteen years. Benefits, of course, begin to accrue during this period. To put off a transformation initiative for another two years is to move two years closer to disaster.

factor of ten in the previous five years; Japanese electronics firms, visiting company representatives discovered, boasted defect rates a thousand times lower than Motorola's.

Motorola's is one of the great success stories of American business, a story of sustained leadership, motivation, worker empowerment, and dogged effort. Between 1986 and 1992, Motorola reduced cost of quality (i.e., the cost of redressing defects) by more than 7 percent of sales, avoiding costs of over $2 billion and garnering the Baldrige Award in the bargain. Sales during this period nearly doubled (sales per employee growing by nearly 80%) with no concomitant price increases, and the company was widely regarded as *the* product innovator in key markets, notably wireless communications.

The most distinctive elements in Motorola's strategy have been its process innovation and commitment to worker education across all activities. The company spends close to 3 percent of sales on education and its Motorola University is widely acclaimed for applying the principles of total quality management to teaching.

Most firms would be delighted to achieve 99.9 percent compliance with quality targets. Motorola, as a reminder that good enough really isn't, emphasizes what 99.9 percent quality means in practice:

- 20,000 wrong drug prescriptions per year;
- unsafe drinking water one hour per month;
- no electricity, water, or heat for approximately nine hours per month;
- 500 incorrect surgical operations per week;
- two close-call landings at major airports per day;
- 2,000 lost mail items per hour.

See also Cost of Quality

Smith, Adam Two centuries after his death, Adam Smith remains one of the most seminal influences on both economics and business. His articulation of the market as the "invisible hand" that maximizes overall social benefits remains the basic statement of the principles of capitalism. Among Smith's other contributions to the fundamentals of management, his identification of division of labor exemplified by the trade of pinmaking as the generator of the "greatest improvement in the productive powers of labor" is today challenged by business process reengineering, which advances alternative bases for organizing work.

See also Business Process Reengineering; Division of Labor; Functional Organization

Standard Deviation

Standard Deviation Standard deviation, the spread of a set of values from its average, is widely used to specify objectives in quality control and quality assurance. Given average production defects of 120 per hundred thousand units, a standard deviation of 25 expresses far greater variability than a standard deviation of 12. Statistical quality control, the foundation of most total quality management techniques, relies on the analysis of output variability to track and resolve problems. It uses standard deviation to determine the percentage of data samples that deviate from the average by a given amount. Two-thirds of all values are within one standard deviation, approximately 95 percent within two standard deviations (see diagram on page 182).

Reducing variability is the key goal of total quality management, as defined by leading gurus and noted company practitioners, and standard deviation is the most accurate measure of variability. Motorola's "six sigma" (the Greek letter sigma is the mathematical term for standard deviation) quality goal translates to less than one defect in three million.

See also Six Sigma Quality; Statistical Quality Control; Total Quality Management (TQM); Variability

Statistical Quality Control

Statistical Quality Control The foundation of the quality movement is to reduce variation from the target standard (e.g., defects per thousand units). Tracking thousands of components,

Adam Smith was and remains among history's greatest thinkers on economics and society. His insights have had long-lasting impacts. To dismiss him as an inconsequential historical figure, as a few "gurus" have, is a little like dismissing Thomas Jefferson as irrelevant to modern times.

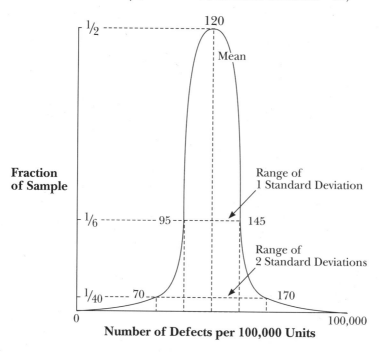

Greater Variability (mean = 120; standard deviation = 25)

Fraction of Sample

1/2 ------ 120
Mean

Range of
1 Standard Deviation

1/6 ---------- 95 ------------ 145

Range of
2 Standard Deviations

1/40 ------ 70 --------------- 170

0

100,000

Number of Defects per 100,000 Units

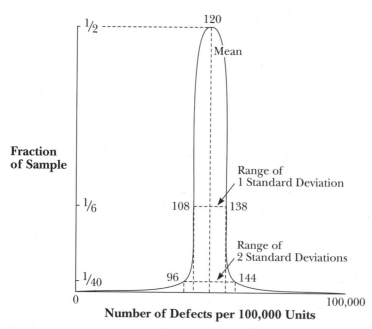

Lower Variability (mean = 120; standard deviation = 12)

Fraction of Sample

1/2 ------ 120
Mean

Range of
1 Standard Deviation

1/6 - 108 ----- 138

Range of
2 Standard Deviations

1/40 - 96 ----- 144

0

100,000

Number of Defects per 100,000 Units

machines, steps, and products requires capturing and processing a huge volume of data in order to monitor performance, diagnose and pinpoint problems, and focus priorities for action. Statistical quality control summarizes these processes of data management. Through such measures as averages, variation (standard deviation), and trend analysis, statistical techniques help imbue volumes of disaggregated numbers with meaning.

Measurement is at the heart of quality. Obviously, choosing exactly what to measure is the challenge.

See also Total Quality Management (TQM); Variability

Stovepipes This term is widely used by proponents of business process reengineering to characterize the traditional functional organization as a set of tightly bounded departments charged with different parts of a process (and likely to view their respective parts as fiefdoms to be defended). The goal of just about every process improvement movement is to dismantle functional stovepipes and redeploy or eliminate their inhabitants.

See also Business Process Reengineering; Functional Organization

Strategic Intent Two professor/consultants coined the term strategic intent to capture the single-minded commitment to a directional target that marks most successful firms. Komatsu's rallying cry, "Surround Caterpillar," is an oft-cited example. It defined no specific strategy for attacking Caterpillar, then the dominant manufacturer of construction equipment, but rather provided a focus for Komatsu's ongoing strategy and tactics. Ford's "Quality is Job 1" similarly clarified strategic priorities for a firm that was failing in its marketplace.

A statement of strategy should make explicit both the few things that really matter (and provide a base for ruthless prioritization) and what a company is *not* going to do. Gary Hamel and C.K. Prahalad, the term's originators, demonstrate clearly that General Motors, Sears, Philips, IBM, Pan Am, and other industry

Even in the early 1990s, with all its talk about teamwork, Ford operated its "chimney" departments almost like independent companies, with separate policies governing pay, promotion, and project assignment. These were the greatest threats to the skunk works unit that successfully rescued the Mustang, at record pace and record cost for launching a new model. A company's most intense competition can be its own organization.

Ample evidence suggests that the single most critical long-term element in competitive success is ruthless prioritization of capital allocation, management direction, and worker effort. Such prioritization is impossible without a clear strategic intent. The previously successful companies that fell into disarray over the past twenty years were strategically adrift. Turnaround, for those that achieved it, was a consequence of strategic clarity and commitment replacing strategic complexity and management diffusion. The bust to boom to bust and back history of Chrysler—and leadership of Lee Iacocca—is marked by busts that sharpen strategic intent and successes that blur it.

leaders were dethroned by want not of strategies and resources (which they possessed in abundance) but of clarity and focus as drivers of strategy. It was strategic drift, in the absence of strategic intent, that felled these leaders.

The process improvement movements, whether directly or indirectly, universally identify strategic intent as a key driver of process innovation. Terminology may vary, but strategic intent, by whatever name it is called—"vision" and top management "commitment" are frequently heard—is a clear statement of direction backed by management behavior that is sufficiently convincing to mobilize and motivate employees. Top management that wants to gauge its own conviction might do well to ask: "What is our firm's strategic intent?"

Taguchi Loss Function   Part of the total quality management vocabulary, the Taguchi loss function was conceived by Japanese quality expert Genichi Taguchi and compatriot Kaoru Ishikawa (who are ranked with Deming and Juran as intellectual leaders in TQM) as a way to characterize the cost of variability in product quality. Taguchi methods emphasize the development of robust designs that are insensitive to uncontrollable factors such as environment or mode of use, addressing aspects of quality that impinge upon cost (e.g., material waste, defects, rework, warranty repairs, dealer training, product replacement, customer support, and so forth) before the designs become operational. However obvious this might seem, a cursory review of the histories of most industries will reveal how radical, in fact, it is.

Recall the traditional U.S. auto industry. Engineering design, production, and sales and finance were separate stovepipes organizationally and locationally distinct in a vertical and functional organization. This structure admitted little discussion at the design stage of, say, dealer education or customer relations. Similarly, traditional banks seldom solicited branch or commercial account rep input prior to launching a new product. This circumstance is amusingly captured by any of the many variations on an old cartoon that depicts the varied, bewildering, and in the end useless constructions that engineering envisioned, production built, and marketing tries to sell to a customer who wants a seesaw.

The Taguchi loss function is a metric. Underlying it is an ethos of quality management that comprises cross-functional teams, sales and production involvement in design, concurrent development, parallelism between sales planning and engineering and production, and customer-driven quality as the basis for *all* planning and implementation.

Taylorism   Frederick Taylor, the turn-of-the-century inventor of "scientific management," is the bête noire of most of the process improvement movements and of the organizational development field that predates them. Taylor, an honorable and caring individual who frequently declined to apply his tools unless workers' wages were increased by as much as 100 percent, does not deserve to be characterized as the embodiment of organizational fascism.

That said, the tools and ethos of scientific management that continue to pervade many companies' assumptions about work, workers, and their management hold efficiency to be the god of business operations and, in so doing, relegate the worker to just another element of efficient, rather than a contributor to effective, operations. Efficiency is concerned with reducing the waste in and cost of processes, effectiveness with choosing the right processes to invest in. To be efficient in the pursuit of the wrong goal is to risk a gentle slide to disaster. Taylor promoted efficiency in a manufacturing environment that was stable and slow to change. He advanced the credo of "one best way" and charged managers to identify it, establish standards and procedures to support it, and train workers to comply with it and reward them for doing so.

In Taylor's schema, managers are thinkers, workers cogs in machines. The former guide the actions of the latter. Most modern management thought and practice turns this schema on its head, holding that the people who do the work know most about

Taylorism is not guilty of heartless disregard for people. Indeed, the successes of lean production, total quality management, and reengineering, direct descendants all of Taylor's scientific management, are almost invariably associated with involving the people who do the work in planning, decision making, and operations.

it. To get results, earn their allegiance and trust and motivate and reward them.

Taylor's belief that statistical and analytic data can yield scientific principles of management—"hard" quantitative relative to "soft" qualitative rules and formulae—also persists today, as the measurement base for management by fact on which much of the quality management movement rests. The field of management science that developed optimization and simulation models is derived from Taylor's scientific management. The radical extremes of business process reengineering are viewed by many as new versions of Taylorism—management's "one best way" implemented at the expense of workers' jobs.

Total Quality Management (TQM) Total quality management (TQM) is the longest-established of all the process movements, with its roots in the work of a number of U.S. and Japanese experts during the 1950s. The Japanese automotive industry was the testbed for the concepts and tools of TQM, with Toyota the main innovator. It was not until the 1980s that U.S. firms adopted TQM, primarily in response to the accelerating success of their Japanese competitors.

TQM is a rigorous discipline, not a rallying cry. Transforming an organization through TQM takes around fifteen years.

TQM then became an overnight fad, with senior executives proclaiming their commitment to quality, even if that commitment remained purely verbal. They appointed relatively junior and often young managers to fill new positions as vice presidents for quality and expected results fast. But many quality programs failed. Without the combination of sustained leadership from the top that marked the successes of firms like Ford, Motorola, and Xerox and genuine empowerment of shop floor workers, TQM amounted to mere words, not deeds.

The deeds require, in the words of W.E. Deming, the patron saint of quality, that "companies drive out fear, so that everyone can work effectively." They also generate stress and fear; the executive responsible for quality at Xerox described the period since the company adopted quality as the driver of its efforts to recover its lost industry leadership as "eleven years of wrenching change." Ironically, one of the managerial goals of TQM being to substantially cut costs, success in quality means loss of jobs. Xerox announced in 1994 that it was reducing its staff once again, by 12 percent. It is difficult for managers to motivate workers to undertake the very hard and disciplined work of transforming quality and then sustaining it through continuous improvement. Xerox found that around six months' time was required to put together a team to implement total quality practices for new products.

TQM is a discipline, rather than a rallying cry or "vision," founded on the following premises:

- *Embrace the long term:* Senior management must take a long-term view and make a long-term commitment to achieving quality. Shortsighted emphasis on short-term, quarterly earnings growth impairs the sustained and continuing improvements needed to transform quality. Popular management books tend to paint a misleading picture of the time frames involved in the successes of Toyota, the most outstanding innovator of the past fifty years; Motorola, the model of quality for American firms; Ford, whose turnaround through quality programs initiated the U.S. fight back against the Japanese car makers; and Xerox, the best-known example of a fight back, through quality, from near disaster. No instant triumphs, these success stories were ten to fifteen years in the making.

- *Empower workers:* Because the people who do the work know that work the best, they need to be empowered to make decisions, whether through quality circles, self-managing teams, manufacturing cells, or other collaborative units. Managers must let go of the notion that management knows best and accept the challenge, and the opportunity, of unleashing the knowledge and creativity of their workers. Such a shift can be made only by building mutual trust and providing incentives. It also requires flexibility in defining jobs—the multiskilled worker replaces specialized division of labor. Companies and unions have had to go through complex and often antagonistic negotiations to achieve the latter. The downsizing, reengineering, leveraged buyouts, and widespread cost-cutting measures of the past decade often continue to hobble worker empowerment.

- *Reduce variability:* "Quality" means a target standard for components and final products, with "zero defects" the ideal. Whereas U.S. practice for decades was to meet a standard that was within a given range (e.g., a component should weigh 3.6 ounces, with the acceptable "within tolerance variation" being 3.47–3.37 ounces [3.6 +/− .13 ounces]), the TQM target is more specific (in this case, 3.6). The TQM goal is not to get, say, 97 percent of components within the range, but to narrow the variability around the target, reducing the numbers of components that deviate from it. The difference is between "good enough" and "meets the target." TQM relies heavily on the collection and interpretation of statistical data to monitor performance, diagnose problems, and take action.

- *Manage by fact:* TQM relies on fact, not opinion, in every element of management. "Quality" is not a qualitative issue but one of precise quantitative metrics. The leaders in quality management monitor in exquisite detail operational measures of quality and let the facts speak for themselves. For instance, each of FedEx's top managers is responsible for an objective quality measure, such as the number of packages that were damaged in transit yesterday. The number may be very small, but that's not the issue. If you neglect the details and look just at the "big picture," you lose quality. The damaged package delivered to customer XYZ may have been the only damaged one of thousands, but to the recipient, it marked a 100 percent failure of quality.

- *Remove waste:* Waste—in materials, time, errors, rework, inventory, and so on—is the enemy. The origins of TQM are closely linked to the just-in-time inventory management techniques pioneered by Toyota to minimize waste and delays in materials management. The goal is to match supply with use, constantly replenishing inventory on an as-needed basis, thus avoiding wasting time because of out-of-stock situations and avoiding wasting money and space because of excess inventory.

- *Generate continuous improvement:* The primary ethos of TQM is continuous improvement. Each word can be emphasized separately: *continuous* improvement, continuous *improvement*. Achieving continuous improvement is a big challenge, but some commentators treat it as ho-hum, arguing that it results only in small-scale, incremental change at a time when firms need to take bold leaps ahead. TQM advocates counter that taking bold leaps doesn't help you run the never-ending race. It's compounding a 10, 12, or 15 percent improvement for ten years that generates the big wins, not a one-shot 40 percent gain.

All this adds up to a rich body of concepts, tools, and techniques. At its worst, TQM can become a metrics bureaucracy and a set of evangelistic clichés about putting the customer first, getting it right the first time, and so on. At its best, it is the foundation for the firm of the 1990s.

That foundation has been built on in many ways. To a large degree, TQM no longer represents the way forward to competitive success but is the essential requirement for being in the game today. In the auto industry, the gap between Japanese and U.S. car makers has been so narrowed that quality is not an advantage—instead, lack of quality is a disadvantage. The move now is to exploit the quality base, through service, time to market, shareholder value.

Today many companies view TQM as part of a broader investment strategy, rather than an end in itself. Florida Power and Light, winner of the Baldrige Award for quality in the United States and the first American firm to win the Japanese Deming Prize for quality, now recognizes that misguided quality efforts can interfere with providing service. After the company abolished its 85-person quality department and 1,500 quality teams, its customer service improved. Other firms are paying increased attention to the trade-off between TQM, which relies on continuous step-by-step improvement in processes, and reengineering, which advocates a radical once-and-for-all scrapping of existing processes. They also look more carefully at the trade-off between TQM and speed. Hewlett-Packard, for instance, now treats TQM just like any other investment opportunity. It must show a fast payoff in terms of sales, customer satisfaction, or cost savings.

See also Agile Manufacturing; Continuous Improvement; Deming, W. Edwards; Kaizen

Toyota's "Five Whys"   Much of the established philosophy and many of the concepts and tools of total quality management emanated from the Japanese automaker Toyota, which also developed just-in-time production, among many other innovations in manufacturing. Toyota's "five whys" are an approach to rooting out the causes of problems by asking a series of questions. Consider, by way of illustration, the example of Taiichi Ohno, the guiding genius of Toyota's quality management program, inquiring about the cause of a machine stoppage.

Question 1:   Why did the machine stop?

Answer 1:   Because the fuse blew due to an overload.

When executives from Detroit's Big Three auto firms tried to identify, and later copy, the "secret" of Toyota's manufacturing processes, what they largely missed was the company's total commitment to solving problems as they occurred (otherwise the entire just-in-time flow stopped dead). One General Motors manager reported to his Toyota counterpart in a joint venture, "No problems." The reply was "No problem is problem." To say that everything is fine means people aren't looking for opportunities for continuous improvements, aren't pursuing kaizen. Toyota's problem-seeking, problem-solving culture

Question 2:   Why was there an overload?

  Answer 2:   Because the bearing lubrication was inadequate.

Question 3:   Why was the lubrication inadequate?

  Answer 3:   Because the lubricating pump was not working right.

Question 4:   Why was the lubricating pump not working right?

  Answer 4:   Because the pump axle was worn out.

Question 5:   Why was the pump axle worn out?

  Answer 5:   Because sludge got in.

Absent the subsequent questions, the workers' natural response would be to change the fuse.

TQM   *See* Total Quality Management

Transaction Costs   One of the most important developments in theoretical work on economics and organization is what is dryly termed transaction cost economics. The notion derives from the work of British economist Ronald Coase, who asked the deceptively simple question, "Why do firms exist?" followed by the more specific question, "What determines which functions a firm keeps in-house and which it buys from the market?" (If all firms bought everything from the market, there would be no firms. If they did everything in-house, they would be like the medieval and imperial economies, dominated by a handful of organizations with no free market.)

The latter question led Coase to posit that companies incur two main types of cost, (1) transaction cost (the price they pay for a good or service) and (2) coordination cost (which includes the costs of administration, management, and information processing). Organizational logic suggests that firms go to market when their coordination costs exceed the market transaction cost and resort to hierarchy when the latter holds. Oliver Williamson,

pervades every function and level. Chrysler's development of its Neon, Ford's launch of its new Mustang, and General Motors' essential resurrection all exploited Toyota's "secrets," successfully only when management made everyone involved responsible for identifying problems and contributing to their resolution.

The make-buy outsource–retain in-house decision is fundamentally a trade-off between transaction costs—what you have to pay someone else—and coordination costs—your costs in management, administration, organization, overhead, and so forth. Transaction costs are easily identified, coordination costs much less so.

the economist who for many years promulgated this message to his peers, coined the phrase "markets and hierarchies" to capture the impact of transaction costs on firms' "economizing," by which he meant organizing their structures and processes to create and sustain wealth.

The distinction between transaction and coordination costs has many practical and useful applications in process innovation. Outsourcing, for example, replaces many internal coordination costs (e.g., of supervision and management and of the people, systems, and technology needed to execute a process) with a transaction cost (e.g., of contracting with another firm to execute the process). Outsourcing is not devoid of coordination costs (e.g., the cost of managing an outsourcing relationship is a coordination cost).

Information technology affects coordination costs in a variety of ways. Computer-to-computer customer-supplier links established to handle ordering, delivery, accounting, and payment (generically referred to as "electronic data interchange"), for example, substitute technology for people costs.

See also Coordination Costs; Outsource

Trust   Trust is the new currency of organizational life. It is a central requirement for many types of process innovation that depend on teamwork and close cooperation. Often, trust must be cultivated in a historical context of distrust. Improving quality, for example, often relies on improving the relationship between a manufacturer and its suppliers in order to facilitate joint efforts to minimize defects and ensure smooth, just-in-time operations. To streamline the distribution chain, retailers must keep key suppliers informed of sales patterns, information previously closely guarded and used as a lever to negotiate prices and terms of supply. Within firms, cross-functional teams must overcome functions' distrust of one another. The healthy impacts of major process innovation that changes the basics of work and, hence, employment will be blocked by management-worker distrust. Partnering efforts by service vendors and their clients will amount to little more than public relations exercises in the absence of trust.

There are two, quite distinct components of trust: trustworthiness and trustability. Trust is a skill as well as a value; trustworthiness is the value part, trustability the skill. To cultivate trust thus requires value—honesty, openness, sincerity—and skill—reliability and dependability. To say "I trust you" must imply both.

Trustworthiness is manifested in sincerity and the honoring of agreements. It can be developed and sustained through personal relationships and track record, or through painstaking crafting of formal contracts designed to avert misunderstandings and provide metrics for ensuring that commitments are met.

Trustability is essential to cross-functional, interorganizational process coordination in a just-in-time environment. Each party must be confident that the other will deliver on time and as specified; both must avoid the dropped-ballerina problem. Operating at the extreme of just in time, ballet companies are ruthless about competence: "If you can't dance, get off the stage" is an oft-reiterated adage. And for good reason. A male dancer who lifts up the ballerina and then drops her onto the stage during a performance of Swan Lake cannot turn to the audience and explain, "Never mind. I'm still at 99.95 percent uptime this performance. Up you get, Vanessa. Maestro, if you'll just go back a few bars, we'll start again." Arts teams are fundamentally concerned with trustability, not trustworthiness. They do not have to (indeed, often may not) like each other in order to collaborate.

In this regard, and as a consequence of cross-functional linkages of processes, just-in-time operations, and customer-supplied electronic links, businesses are becoming more and more like arts teams. As processes are designed or redesigned to eliminate waste and delays and the activities and players become more tightly coupled and highly interdependent, breakdowns in one part of the process immediately affect the other parts.

Much of the management literature on reengineering, total quality management, customer-supplier links, and other process

Historically, retailers and manufacturers have closely guarded information about their suppliers' sales, quality, usage, and so forth in order to have the upper hand in contract negotiations. The relationship was basically one of mutual distrust. The new core of joint management of the supply chain is trust. Management-employee relations in large U.S. firms exhibit a similar pattern of mutual distrust. Nearly every documented turnaround of a failing American giant has relied on rebuilding lost trust. That trust can neither be faked nor implanted by words and rallying cries about teamwork is all too evident in the awful story of General Motors through the early 1990s.

initiatives that rely on cooperation and collaboration presumes mutual trust between actors but neglects entirely its cultivation. Yet these almost invariably generate distrust. Reductions in staff, for example, are an inevitable consequence of reengineering. "Empowering" workers in this context as part of the reengineering "team" without making it clear in advance that loss of jobs may be or even is intended to be the outcome is both demoralizing and unjust. "Downsizing," however necessary and urgent management might perceive it to be, is likely to be construed by loyal workers as a breach of trust that will predispose them to doubt the sincerity of future management pronouncements. Well-publicized examples abound of loss of trust impeding the ability of firms to make changes essential to their business survival. General Motors under Chairman Roger Smith was, for example, a regime of massive process innovation and massive resistance not to change but to management.

A supplier that can't deliver on time and quality won't be trusted. An unreliable and incompetent department won't be a welcome addition to a cross-functional team. The functional stovepipes, fragmented activities, delays, waste, and excess inventories disdained by the process movements had the advantage of reducing interdependencies and the impact of time on performance. Incompetent, unreliable departments didn't drag competent, reliable ones down with them, and ample inventory stock covered late deliveries.

In the process of compiling this glossary, the authors encountered numerous articles and books dealing with partnership, teams, and the need for trust but practically none about building trust. Extensive experience with companies pursuing process innovation has convinced the authors that trust or lack thereof is absolutely at the core of the relationships companies are trying to forge. The absence of discussion of "trust processes" is puzzling. What sense does it make to presume trust in the absence of knowledge of how to build it, or for the untrustable to demand trust?

Managers considering major process changes need to answer the following questions.

- Which relationships are key (e.g., between us as management and our staff; between us as a vendor/supplier and our clients and customers)?

- Are we perceived by our partners to be trustworthy? How are we regarded by prospective partners, competitors, clients, and customers? Do we fulfill our promises, advertising claims, announced plans?

- Are our partners trustworthy? Do we really want to work with them if they are not? Are the proposed process changes realistic? Are formal contracts needed or desirable?

- Are we trustable, i.e., so competent in *all* the processes relevant to ensuring trust in the relationship that the others in the relationship can rely on us? (What about our billing system? The legal department's handling of contracts? Fairness of bonus program? Speed in completing paperwork?)

- Are our partners so competent in *all* the processes relevant to ensuring trust in their relationship with us?

Process innovations that depend on trust relationships greatly raise the stakes for all involved. Trustworthiness demands high standards of business ethics and frankness. *Trustability* demands total competence.

Trust is more than words.

UNIX   UNIX is the computer operating system most widely used to support information technology–based reengineering of customer service processes, particularly those that rely on existing computer systems built around functional and departmental processes that cannot be quickly or inexpensively replaced. Front-

The entire thrust of information technology today is to put computer power at the user's fingertips—on the engineer's or customer agent's desktop, in the briefcase, at the point-of-sale terminal, in the travel agency. The UNIX operating system is the "heart" of many of these systems. Its computational efficiency, programmer flexibility, and other technical features are purchased at the cost of usability, reflecting the essential and inevitable trade-off in the choice of operating system for a personal computer or workstation.

ending them with UNIX-based workstations can transform older systems into powerful, easy-to-use customer service tools. The emergence of UNIX as the tool of choice for business is rooted in pragmatism.

- Many computer vendors' UNIX workstations exploit a hardware development termed RISC (for Reduced Instruction Set Computing) that greatly reduces the cost of providing computer speed and power.

- UNIX was the first desktop operating system to support "multitasking," the running of more than one software program at the same time. Thus, a workstation could process a customer transaction, update account information, and prepare billing instructions simultaneously.

- UNIX is associated with both the newer computer programming languages that facilitate highly efficient (and hence rapid) design and implementation of desktop systems and the new generation of clever programmers who use them.

- Perhaps most important, UNIX incorporates a telecommunications protocol (a set of conventions and procedures for linking multiple computer systems) that, albeit somewhat inefficient, greatly reduces the difficulty of getting software systems that run on different computers to communicate.

These characteristics and capabilities seem to have been deemed by business to balance the operating system's arcane complexity and limited provisions for security and management control. Although UNIX itself is not particularly easy to use, it provides a technical base for developing workstations that are. Over time, it is likely to be displaced. Current contenders among the newer generation of operating systems include IBM's OS/2 and Microsoft's family of Windows products (e.g., NT and Chicago).

From the perspective of process innovation, the importance of UNIX, OS/2, and Windows is that effective process design begins at the customer contact point, which increasingly is the workstation. The agent at that contact point must be able to access information and transaction processing systems simply and quickly. The technology of a business process must thus be focused on its contact point.

See also Front-Ending

Value Builders   Value builders are a menu of proven options that increase the economic value-added of a business process. They include many of the tools of business process reengineering, total quality management, and other process movements. In the Business Process Investment framework, the term value builder is used to highlight issues that are key to getting the process right.

There is and can be no one "best" way of improving a process. Each of the process movements has its own goals and techniques that reflect on those goals. Business process reengineering, for instance, seeks radical change, and its tools emphasize, as the term reengineering suggests, using industrial engineering techniques to streamline and hub workflows. Total quality management aspires to continuous incremental improvement; its tools focus on streamlining processes. The learning organization aims to position a company for adaptation and innovation in an era of increasing change and flexibility; its process improvement efforts center around collaboration and teams rather than workflows. *All* of these processes are options for a firm.

As the main criterion for process investment, value is an economic concept of business processes as capital assets and liabilities. It is not the same as benefit; streamlining a process by taking out waste, reducing delays, and cutting staff may or may not generate the most value for the firm. The choice of value builder is thus a management decision.

Accordingly, the menu of value builders developed for the

Abandoning travel expense reporting, outsourcing management accounting, reengineering insurance policy issuing, hubbing customer service, turning a telephone call billing system into a product, using an airline reservation system to preempt hotel chains' control of their own product—all of these are ways to extract more value from processes by building on assets, or transforming liability into asset processes. Reengineering, downsizing, and streamlining are among the options on this menu. Treating any one of these as the solution prejudges the problem or opportunity, falls into the one size—and budget—fits all trap.

Business Process Investment framework is a list, derived from case examples, of a wide range of options to which you can add on the basis of your own firm's experience and insights. The sequence is from simple (options that involve limited investment, change, effort, and risk) to complex (those at the other extreme).

- Abandon: Eliminate the process (Shell Europe abandoned travel expense account reporting)

- Outsource: Move the process to a firm for which it is an identity asset process (Laura Ashley outsourced inventory management and distribution to FedEx)

- Front-end: Leave the major part of the process and supporting computer transaction processing systems as is, using computer workstations and telecommunications to add flexibility and new services at the front end and gradually erode the back end (Bell Atlantic invested $2.1 billion to front-end its customer ordering systems to provide near-immediate installation of new services)

- Self-source: Do it yourself or have the customer do it (banks installed ATMs; restaurants set up salad bars; management encouraged employees' use of laptop computers to produce their own presentation graphics and attractively formatted reports)

- Streamline: Tighten linkages between activities and eliminate waste, steps, delays, costs, and people (Toyota used lean production manufacturing processes to reduce by one-half its space requirements, investment in tools, engineering hours, and on-site inventory)

- Hub: Bring work and information to a single customer contact point at which a process can be handled in its entirety (Mutual Benefit reduced processing time from around three weeks to two to four hours by having a case manager handle all the steps involved in issuing a new policy)

- Collaborate: Cultivate a culture and an ethos of cooperation in order to coordinate smooth and effective interactions between interdependent workers (Cemex taught its sales and production staff to work together to remove the barriers of understanding and functional priorities that impeded customer service)

- Worknet: Provide communications infrastructures that enable individuals, groups, and outside firms to coordinate flexibly and collaboratively, and provide training, incentives, and team support for them to do so (Digital Equipment used networks as the base for worldwide, rapid building of teams for special projects and problem solving)

- Import: Adopt a process or process infrastructure from another industry (the State of Maryland issued benefits cards that enable holders to withdraw their welfare benefit payments from banking ATMs and to deduct the cost of food from their accounts via credit card payment authorization terminals in supermarkets)

- Productize: Turn a process into a product that earns money (MCI Communications turned its own customer billing process for long-distance phone calls into a $2-billion-a-year product, "Friends and Family")

- Franchise: Market a process, with supporting expertise, for someone else to turn into a business (McDonald's provided franchises with complete process capability under the McDonald's organizational brand)

- Radicalize: Raise the salience of a process in order to accelerate the degree and pace of organizational change, transform it, or do both (Ford instituted its "Quality is Job 1" slogan)

- Preempt: Use a process infrastructure to capture another industry's traditional business at a customer moment of

value (British Airways usurped international hotels'
control of distribution of their own product by adding
hotel reservations to its airline reservation system)

- Invent: Create a new process by thinking in new ways and
breaking from conceptions of an industry "core" process
(Dell Computer substituted catalogs, telephone ordering,
customized assembly, and UPS delivery for physical stores
and inventory in the retailing of personal computers)

See also Business Process Reengineering; Total Quality Management (TQM); Worth-Salience Matrix

Value Chain　Economist/business strategist Michael Porter argues that there are just two types of competitive advantage: low
cost and differentiation. He developed the concept of the value
chain to help firms determine precisely the degree to which each
impinges their respective competitive positioning.

Substitute in Porter's summary of the value chain concept
"business processes" for "activities" (Porter views the latter as
narrower in focus than functions and departments and also highlights activity linkages, that is, cross-functional processes, as the
core of just-in-time production and time-based competition).

Competitive strategy is manifested in the discrete *activities* a
company performs in competing in a particular business. Activities such as order processing, process design, repair, and sales
force operations are narrower than functions (e.g., marketing,
production). A strategy is reflected in an internally consistent
configuration of activities that is different from that of rivals.
Activities are the ultimate *source* of competitive advantage. Cost
advantage arises because a firm can cumulatively perform the
discrete activities in a business more efficiently. Differentiation
depends instead on a firm's ability to perform particular activities in unique ways that create buyer value. (Michael E. Porter,
"Competitive Strategy Revisited: A View from the 1990s," in *The
Relevance of a Decade: Essays to Mark the First Ten Years of the
Harvard Business School Press,* ed. Paula Barker Duffy [Boston:

*The value chain is
traditionally defined from
the firm's perspective,
beginning with raw
materials and production
and moving through
sales and logistics to the
customer (follow the
arrow from company to
customer). Surely it must
point the other way,
begin with the customer;
the value chain is really
the customer gratification
chain.*

Harvard Business School Press, 1994], 266.)

The diagram below depicts the generic Porter value chain.

Immensely influential in business schools, the information services profession, and business strategy consulting and planning, Porter's model provides a useful framework for pinpointing strengths and weaknesses in a firm's operations and targeting opportunities for improvement. It affords the information systems function a straightforward way to think about using information technology to streamline and integrate, from inbound logistics (electronic customer-supplier links, electronic data interchange), to operations, which is to say, production and service (just-in-time everything), to outbound logistics (telecommunications-based logistics), to marketing and sales and after-sale logistics (information-based planning and customer management).

Porter's framework and the thinking that underlies it are not without limitations. The first one is that, as economists are wont to do, Porter views the customer from the perspective of the firm;

The Porter Value Chain

SUPPORT ACTIVITIES					
Firm Infrastructure e.g., financing, planning, investor relations					
Human Resource Management e.g., recruiting, training, compensation system					
Technology Development e.g., product design, process design, market research, material research					
Procurement e.g., raw materials, advertising space, health services					
Inbound Logistics e.g., data collection, material storage, customer access	**Operations** e.g., component molding, branch operations, underwriting	**Outbound Logistics** e.g., order processing, warehousing, report preparation	**Marketing and Sales** e.g., sales, proposal writing, advertising, trade shows	**After-sale Logistics** e.g., installation, customer support, repair	M A R G I N

PRIMARY ACTIVITIES

Source: Reprinted with the permission of The Free Press, an imprint of Simon & Schuster Inc. from *Competitive Advantage: Creating and Sustaining Superior Performance* by Michael E. Porter. Copyright © 1985 by Michael E. Porter.

hence, arrows in the value chain point left to right, from company to customer. From a process innovation perspective, it makes more sense to reverse the direction, to start from the customer's request and work back. The Porter value chain being fixed, it does not admit opportunities to invent new activities and activity linkages.

Finally, Porter holds that industry is the basic unit of analysis in business strategy. Indeed, the central model from which he derived the value chain is called the Five Forces of Industry Competition. Using existing value chains to intrude on other industries is among the fastest growing trends in process innovation and the one likely to have the most far-reaching impact. Thus, among the leaders in credit cards are AT&T, Sears, and Citibank, with General Motors a strong player, and in providing full-service banking without branches, USAA (insurance), Fidelity Investments, and Merrill Lynch (securities). Ford and General Motors are the largest holders of consumer loan debt. All of these are effectively "banking" firms. The notion of "industry" is becoming increasingly obsolete and self-limiting in the sense that it discourages firms from thinking more broadly about their and their current and potential competitors' value chains.

That said, Porter's model remains influential and useful. It can be rendered more useful by reversing the arrows and asking, "What is our customer's value chain from the first awareness of us and first contact point back through our logistical chain?" and "Where can we invent new value linkages?"

Variability   The core logic of the total quality management movement as applied to manufacturing is that the goal of management and the task of the workers who understand the process is to reduce variability, principally through the collection and analysis of data. Variability is measured against standards, the main statistical measure being the standard deviation. The standard deviation is the range of values of a sample of results that deviate from the average value; two-thirds of the sample fall within one standard deviation, about 95 percent within two standard deviations.

The mathematical term for the standard deviation is the Greek letter sigma, hence Motorola's famous goal of six sigma quality: that its products would deviate from the target standard for quality by fewer than six standard deviations (i.e., only one in six million would not meet the standard). W. Edwards Deming, the strongest proponent of reliance on statistical data as the core of quality management, viewed variability as the single biggest impediment to ensuring quality.

The key to reducing variability and ensuring uniformity is to track what TQM calls process variation (which is measured against a target measure), not which outputs meet specifications. Traditional manufacturing methods would rank a plant that met output specifications 100 percent of the time above one that achieved a 0.3 percent "out of spec" rate. This was the case for two Sony plants. The one that met specifications 100 percent of the time was in San Diego, the other in Japan. The diagram below plots the statistical distribution of the two plants' outputs.

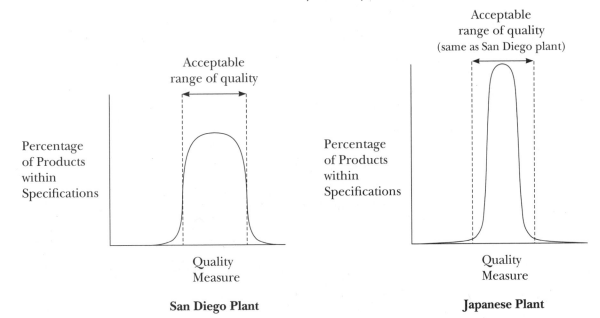

Variability in Sony Plants

San Diego Plant

Japanese Plant

The assumption that meeting specifications satisfies quality targets ignores two factors. One, to be 100 percent "within specification" means that all the products were just "OK." There is no incentive to examine process details and pursue improvements. Although a plant that is 100 percent within spec might seem to be more efficient than one that is, say, 92 percent within spec, such might not be the case as the diagram illustrates. The San Diego plant's performance rarely leaves the range of acceptable performance; that production is well within "tolerance" limits translates to "we can tolerate this." The plant exhibits far more variability than does the Japanese plant. Variability translates (explicitly so in the language of the total quality management movement) to "this is within conformance." Is the more appropriate metric of quality "tolerance limits" or "degree of conformance?" What do leading TQM gurus think?

- "I define quality as conformance to requirements. Period. We should perform the job or produce the product as we agreed to do it." (Philip Crosby, *Quality Is Free: The Art of Making Quality Free* [Milwaukee: American Society for Quality Control, 1979].)

- "Good quality does not necessarily mean high quality. It means a predictable degree of uniformity and dependability at low cost with a quality suited to the market." (W.E. Deming, *Out of the Crisis* [Milwaukee: American Society for Quality Control, 1986].)

The TQM focus on management by fact and use of statistical information has prompted thoughtful emphasis on suitable metrics. As illustrated by the Sony example, what you choose to measure strongly influences motivation, incentives, attitude, and interpretation of results. Obviously, a focus on variability is best suited to processes that generate a standard product or support a highly standardized service, such as FedEx's package operations (each FedEx top manager is responsible for a performance metric and all managers' bonuses depend on meeting or beating targets; FedEx is a process driven and, thus, metric-driven firm).

Many of the process improvement movements aim at increasing flexibility and adaptability and, thus, to some extent, variability. These tend to highlight how employees have dealt with some exceptional situation, a frequent feature of American Express ads. What metrics capture performance under these circumstances? The TQM movement has made reduction of variability a primary target and, hence, metric for which the principal competitive driver is Deming's "*predictable* degree of *uniformity* and *dependability* at *low cost* with a quality suited to the market" (emphasis added). For services that depend on flexibility, the driver might be "predictable degree of *responsiveness* and *assurance of meeting the customer request* at *fair* cost."

The variability/flexibility trade-off, being to some extent a trade-off between low cost and competitive differentiation, the two main sources of competitive advantage, is likely to be one of the most difficult issues for process innovation in coming years.

See also Cause-and-Effect Diagrams; Standard Deviation

Virtual Corporation   A virtual *product* is one that can be made available at any time, in any place, and in any variety. A virtual *corporation,* according to William Davidow and Michael Malone, authors of an influential 1992 book by that title, is a technology-driven company structured around alliances with partners and suppliers and the outsourcing of operations that provides customized services and products on demand.

The virtual corporation employs a small core of people focused on its central strategic priorities and contracts physical operations to other firms. The concept of the virtual firm is in many ways a consolidation of many strands of the process movements: time as the key element in getting to market; close, trust-based relationships with suppliers; speed and flexibility of opera-

Telecommunications makes work time- and location-independent. Customer service, field sales, manufacturing, distribution, and other functions needn't be in the same location, organization, or time zone. Telecommunications networks make possible the virtual corporation; trust and collaboration turn that possibility into reality. The result is a growing variety of organizational options that combine flexibility, speed of response, low cost, and high service. The process-defined, not structure-dependent, organization is the emerging blueprint for process design.

The "networked" organization depends as much on collaboration and communication as on enabling technology. IBM and GM had plenty of enterprise networks; what they lacked were enterprise worknets to supplant their functional and divisional fiefdoms.

The workstation is the access point to services and the focal point for bringing together the information needed to deliver those services. The more powerful a workstation, the more services it can access and support. The personal computer and its technical variants are the workstations of today; the telephone, wireless personal communication devices, and interactive television, which have the advantage of extensive reach and universal availability and ubiquity, are among the likely workstations of tomorrow.

tions as the driving and binding organizational force; and value- rather than price-based marketing.

"Virtual" is widely used in the computer field to define a system or resource in terms of its performance and the user's perspective. Tricks of the software trade might, for example, enable a computer with 16 million bytes of internal memory to run programs as large as 8 billion bytes. Such a computer is said to have a physical memory of 16 million and a virtual memory of 8 billion bytes.

Virtual organization thus contrasts with traditional physical organization. A growing number of examples of corporations well along the scale from physical to virtual firm includes Verifone, the predominant supplier of credit card readers, which substitutes worldwide electronic mail for a head office and staff and for such activities as hiring, budgeting, and reporting financial results.

Worknet   Michael Schrage, a writer on collaboration, coined the term worknet to distinguish between a network that provides the base for communication, and the community and culture that do the communicating. The combination of a technology for communication and culture for communicating constitutes a worknet.

Workstation   Technically, a workstation is a personal computer-like device loaded up with computer chips and software and provided with telecommunications capabilities. In practice, it's the same as a personal computer from the user's perspective.

One of the key building blocks for using information technology as a cornerstone for process improvement, workstations provide a "front end" that enables complex processing systems and information resources to be accessed quickly and simply. Workstations handle the organization of inputs, communication with multiple systems, and formatting and display of outputs. Workstations are used by a variety of workers for many different functions: travel agents for making reservations, engineers for designing products, and adjusters for processing insurance claims. The more processing power their workstations have, the faster the users can work and the more information they can process.

Worth/Salience Matrix The Worth/Salience matrix, shown below, is used in conjunction with the Business Process Investment framework to classify business processes in terms of relative economic value to a firm (i.e., worth) and relative importance in terms of impact on the factors that most affect strategy and

Which processes are most central to a firm's success and failure? Which generate, and which drain, value? Which are economic assets and which liabilities? Answering these questions is the key to identifying the right process to get right and targeting resources accordingly.

WORTH

	ASSET	LIABILITY

SALIENCE

Identity
Defines the firm to
its customers,
itself, and its investors

Priority
Drives everyday
performance and
competitive success

Background
Provides everyday
operations for support
of other activities

Mandated
Performed
to comply
with legalities
and regulations

Folklore
Carried out for
the sake of a
rigid tradition

competitive positioning (i.e., salience). A detailed summary of Business Process Investment is provided in the Introduction.

One of the most difficult tasks of process innovation is to identify which processes represent competitive opportunities or necessities. Which of a firm's typically hundreds of business processes exert the greatest impact on its current, future, and potential fortunes? By and large, the process improvement movements do not answer this question convincingly. Some by their very conception predefine the process to get right. Most stress the importance of processes that most directly affect customers. Total quality management, for example, targets processes that generate products and services that customers purchase. Reengineering does likewise, implicitly emphasizing processes that are key to success and in poor shape (the very term reengineering signals repair and renovation). These are often termed "core" processes, which reengineering/redesign advocates believe average from ten to twenty in the typical firm.

These criteria for selecting targets of opportunity—core process and impact on customers—filter out other processes. If they are the most appropriate criteria, they filter out processes that are less relevant to success. It's hard to argue that processes that do not directly affect customer service or product quality and that are not core to the business should take precedence, but this is precisely what the Worth/Salience matrix frequently indicates to firms. This is not to suggest that customer service and product quality are not of critical importance, rather that it is vital that other potentially important processes not be screened out before they can be identified. The discussion of the process paradox in the Introduction and under its own entry, cites examples of firms that won the Baldrige Award for quality in "core" manufacturing operations, yet failed miserably in leadership, pricing, employee relations, and capital resource allocation processes. Also cited are instances of successful process innovations that generate substantial benefits in terms of time, cost, staff, and error reduction, yet do not precipitate overall improvements in a business unit's financial performance.

The Worth/Salience matrix can help firms avoid the process paradox. It views business processes as economic assets and liabilities directly analogous to R&D, a long-term capital investment that does not appear on the balance sheet. Capital invested in business processes constitutes a comparable long-term resource that does not show up on the balance sheet. Asset and liability processes are thus those that tie up substantial financial capital vis-à-vis long-term investment in people (recruitment, training, support), facilities, technology (development, operations and maintenance of computer systems, piloting of new systems, and so on), investment of management time and attention (including planning reengineering projects), and other types of cost typically expensed or not seen as directly part of process capital.

Business Process Investment defines process's worth as follows.

- An asset process uses the capital invested in it to create economic value-added (EVA). It does so by (1) directly generating value by differentiating the company in the marketplace or providing it with a cost and pricing advantage (as by emphasizing production quality, customer service, product development, investment management, or distribution processes); (2) preserving value by ensuring that the firm maintains its distinctive differentiation (as through leadership and management development, recruitment, acquisition, financing, branding, or advertising processes); or (3) enabling the creation of new value (as through investment in infrastructures such as global telecommunications, basic research, recruitment, team-building, organizational design, and incentive processes).

- A liability process, however well performed, drains value from a firm. It consumes capital without generating economic value-added. Processing payroll is a liability process in this sense, as are many regulatory compliance and reporting processes and most "administrative" processes (e.g., expense account reporting).

- A value-neutral process is one that is expense only. It does not tie up capital and can be largely ignored as a target of opportunity for process innovation (although clearly a firm should, in the interest of efficiency, try to cut its costs wherever it can).

Note that this view of processes highlights those—management development, finance, recruiting, and team-building, for example—filtered out by the process improvement movements that focus on workflows and customer-centered or core processes. The worth component of the Worth/Salience matrix asks the simple question, "Which processes have we invested our capital in and do they create or drain value?"

The salience component expands the question to "Which of these processes are most important relative to our strategic business priorities?" The Business Process Investment framework defines five categories of salience.

1. *Identity processes.* These define a firm to its customers, itself, and its investors. Think of FedEx and you think of guaranteed, on-time, overnight delivery. Think of your firm and you think of . . . ?

2. *Priority processes.* Firms that handle these, the engines of everyday performance in the marketplace, better than their competitors have a distinct edge. When these processes fail, customers feel the impact and management worries.

3. *Background processes.* These accounting, administrative, and other "overhead" processes are literally part of a company's background.

4. *Mandated processes.* These are the tax compliance and other processes that firms carry out because they must.

5. *Folklore processes.* These are the processes carried out for the sake of a rigid tradition.

Classifying processes in terms of worth and salience provides a basis for determining which processes to invest in and choosing a process value builder. The various process improvement movements provide tools for building asset, or transforming liability into asset, processes, but they generally either present them as *the* solution regardless of process, or focus only on the type of process to which they are suited. Thus, proponents of radical reengineering, employing as value builders primarily some form of streamlining and reorientation toward the customer, target only liability processes. Total quality management emphasizes building and maintaining the value of asset processes through continuous incremental improvement. Advocates of downsizing, the virtual corporation, alliances, and teams advance their respective single solutions in the contexts in which they apply. The logic of the Worth/Salience approach is to first choose the process to get right and then choose the solution that makes sense in terms of improving worth, salience, or, ideally, both.

The Business Process Investment framework offers some guiding principles.

- Identity asset processes are sources of long-term, value-generating differentiation. Protect them. In the absence of such processes, a company is limited to a "me-too" strategy.

- Radically and urgently reengineer identity liability and priority processes. These are what kill a company.

- Invest in continuous improvement of priority asset processes.

- Outsource background and mandated liability processes, but only to a firm for which they are identity asset processes.

A firm, whether it applies the Worth/Salience logic or not, must have a clear basis for choosing which processes to improve. In this capacity, nearly all the process improvement movements are limited and limiting. Managers are well advised to attend to the following dangers.

- Reengineering and total quality management generally highlight processes with well-defined workflows and overlook "soft" processes (although their insights are gradually permeating the field of organizational behavior).

- Reengineering concepts and tools are likely to lead managers to invest in background liability processes and thus generate abundant benefits from processes that, being neither priority nor identity, exert limited impact on value for the firm.

- Downsizing and outsourcing are often viewed only in terms of cost. Determinants of which processes to outsource are capital (worth) and relative impact on strategic value-generating capabilities (salience).

- The typical firm hasn't a clue how much capital is tied up in its processes and so has no real basis for deciding where to direct investments in innovation and improvement.

See also Background Processes; Core Process; Identity Processes; Mandated Processes; Process Paradox; Value Builders

Index

About the Authors

Peter G.W. Keen is the chairman of the International Center for Information Technologies. *Information Week* identified him as one of the top ten consultants in the information technology field. He has worked on an ongoing basis with managers in such firms as British Airways, the Royal Bank of Canada, Cemex (Mexico), Citibank, MCI, and the General Accounting Office. Keen's research, writing, teaching, and consulting focus on bridging the worlds and cultures of business and IT. He has written ten books on the link between IT and business strategy and policy.

Ellen M. Knapp is the vice chairman of technology at Coopers & Lybrand and chairman of the firm's International Technology Management Group. Previously, she was national director of C&L's Information Technology Consulting practice. Knapp has provided both technical and management consulting services to a wide range of public and private sector clients, including transnational consumer products companies, large service sector organizations, and worldwide manufacturing enterprises, and has served as a speaker or moderator at numerous symposia in both the United States and Europe.